Southern Living
HOLIDAYS &
CELEBRATIONS

Editor-in-Chief: Nancy J. Fitzpatrick
Senior Foods Editor: Susan Carlisle Payne
Senior Editor, Editorial Services: Olivia Kindig Wells
Art Director: James Boone

SouthernLiving® Holidays & Celebrations

Editor: Julie Fisher
Designers: Elizabeth Passey Edge, Emily Albright
Copy Editor: Donna Baldone
Editorial Assistant: Lisa C. Bailey
Foods Editor: Cathy A. Wesler
Director, Test Kitchens: Vanessa Taylor Johnson
Assistant Director, Test Kitchens: Gayle Hays Sadler
Test Kitchen Home Economists: Beth Floyd, Michele
    Brown Fuller, Elizabeth Luckett, Christina A. Pieroni,
    Kathleen Royal, Angie Neskaug Sinclair, Jan A. Smith
Senior Photographer: Jim Bathie
Senior Photo Stylist: Kay E. Clarke
Prop Assistant: Connie Formby
Production and Distribution Manager: Phillip Lee
Associate Production Manager: Theresa L. Beste
Production Assistant: Marianne Jordan
Creative Consultants: Melisa Buchanan, Ann Cain

Cover: Fudge Pie with Peanut Butter Sauce (page 103)
Pictured at Right: Praline Wafers (page 26)
Previous Page: Birthday Cake Laced with Love (page 97)
Back Cover: Tenderloin for Two with Peppercorn Cream,
    Green Beans with Crispy Shallots (page 102)

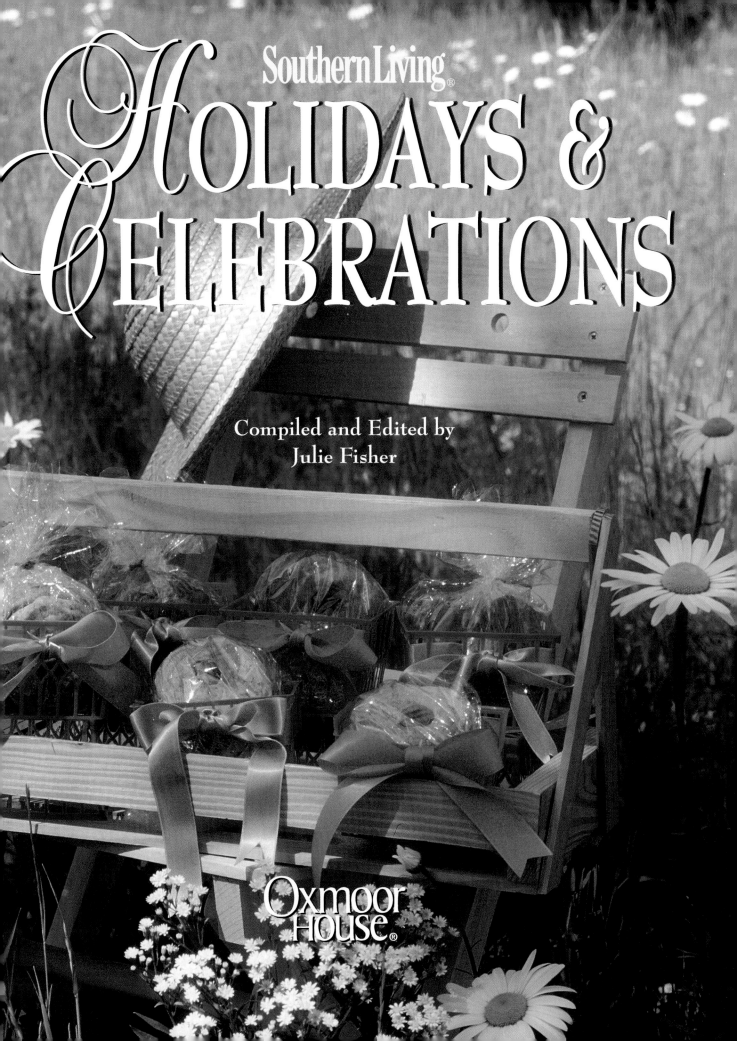

Southern Living®

Holidays & Celebrations

Compiled and Edited by
Julie Fisher

Oxmoor
House®

C O N T

page 10

To the world's greatest Dad!

page 47

page 83

E N T S

page 108

page 100

page 128

page 148

I O N *T*his is a book of celebration that gives you a year's worth of inspiration for entertaining family and friends. Presented in four seasonal chapters, the themed events and recipes emphasize the most enjoyable aspects of each season.

For carefree entertaining, the menus include a combination of original recipes and commercial items that are readily available at your local market. The recipes combine classic ingredients with a twist for unforgettable flavor and presentation. And you'll find more than great recipes here.

- Color photographs bring the menus to life and highlight unique entertaining ideas.
- Details for developing party themes are introduced by the symbol ✦.
- Special projects and gifts of food are found on *Potpourri* pages.
- Easy ways to adapt themed menus to fit other occasions are suggested as **Party Options**.

Together, the recipes, photographs, and party suggestions will enable you to transform any event into the most memorable celebration.

page 31

page 28

I N G

An Easter Feast

Serves 8

Cranberry Ham

Honey-and-Nut Rice

Steamed Broccoli Spears

Sweet Potato Biscuits

Easter Egg Custard Ring

Iced Tea   Coffee

Easter is a time to savor the promise of new life, evidenced by spring as it blossoms on the heels of winter. Gather your family for this noonday feast—make it a springtime version of Thanksgiving. Decorate your dining room with a display of tulips, dogwood blossoms, and Easter bonnets poised on hat stands. Set your table with a pastel theme; mix and match colors of iced tea glasses and ribbons that tie goodies to each place setting (see page 13).

Clockwise from top: Sweet Potato Biscuits (page 14), Honey-and-Nut Rice (page 13), Cranberry Ham (page 12), steamed broccoli spears

Cranberry Ham

1 (5- to 7-pound) smoked fully
   cooked ham half
  Whole cloves
1 (8-ounce) can jellied cranberry sauce
¼ cup firmly packed brown sugar
3 tablespoons cider vinegar
1 tablespoon commercial steak sauce
½ teaspoon dry mustard
¼ teaspoon ground allspice
¼ teaspoon ground cloves
2 tablespoons orange juice
1 bunch red grapes
  Garnish: salad savoy

Remove and discard skin from ham. Score fat on ham in a diamond design, and stud with whole cloves. Place ham, fat side up, on a rack in a shallow roasting pan. Insert meat thermometer, making sure it does not touch fat or bone.

Combine cranberry sauce and next 6 ingredients, stirring well. Baste ham lightly with cranberry mixture. Cover and bake at 325° for 1 hour. Uncover and baste ham Bake, uncovered, an additional hour or until meat thermometer registers 140°, basting every 15 minutes.

Combine orange juice and remaining cranberry mixture in a skillet. Trim grapes to make several small clusters. Add grapes to orange juice mixture; toss gently. Cook over low heat just until grapes are glazed.

Transfer ham to a serving platter. Add glazed grapes. Garnish, if desired. Yield: 10 to 14 servings.

Note: Chop leftover ham, and toss with any leftover Honey-and-Nut Rice. Cover and chill. Serve as a main-dish salad in Bibb lettuce cups.

Polka-Dot Eggs

◆ *Children will enjoy making these fanciful polka-dot eggs. Simply apply self-adhesive round labels to dry hard-cooked eggs. Dip eggs in dye; let dry completely, and peel off labels.*

Honey-and-Nut Rice

1 cup sliced celery
¾ cup chopped onion
2 tablespoons butter or margarine
3½ cups cooked long-grain rice
1 cup coarsely chopped walnuts, toasted
⅓ cup raisins
⅓ cup golden raisins
3 tablespoons honey
3 tablespoons lime juice
1 tablespoon olive oil
¼ teaspoon salt
¼ teaspoon ground cinnamon
¼ teaspoon pepper
  Garnish: celery leaves

Sauté celery and onion in butter in a Dutch oven until vegetables are tender. Remove from heat. Add rice, walnuts, and raisins, stirring well.

Combine honey, lime juice, olive oil, salt, cinnamon, and pepper in a small bowl; stir well. Drizzle honey mixture over rice. Toss gently. Spoon into a serving bowl. Garnish, if desired. Yield: 8 to 10 servings.

Sweet Potato Biscuits

2 cups self-rising flour
3 tablespoons brown sugar
¼ teaspoon ground allspice
¼ cup butter or margarine
3 tablespoons butter-flavored
   shortening
1 cup mashed, cooked sweet potato
¼ cup plus 2 tablespoons milk
2 tablespoons butter or margarine,
   melted

Combine first 3 ingredients in a bowl. Cut in ¼ cup butter and shortening with a pastry blender until mixture is crumbly. Add sweet potato and milk, stirring just until dry ingredients are moistened. Turn dough out onto a floured surface; knead 3 or 4 times.

Roll dough to ½-inch thickness; cut with a 2-inch biscuit cutter. Place biscuits on an ungreased baking sheet. Brush with melted butter. Bake at 400° for 12 minutes. Yield: 1½ dozen.

Jelly Bean Baskets

◆ *Fill miniature wicker Easter baskets with multicolored jelly beans wrapped in plastic wrap. Tie colored ribbons to basket handles and then to napkins at each place setting.*

Easter Egg Custard Ring

2 cups half-and-half
1 (14-ounce) can sweetened
   condensed milk
⅓ cup milk
1 vanilla bean, split
   lengthwise
3 large eggs, beaten
2 egg yolks, beaten
2 cups pastel-colored, egg-shaped
   malted milk candies
Rich Chocolate Sauce

Combine first 3 ingredients in a nonalu minum saucepan. Scrape vanilla bean seed into milk mixture. Bring mixture to a sim mer over medium heat, stirring constantly.

Combine eggs and yolks in a small bowl Gradually add one-fourth of hot milk mix ture to eggs, stirring constantly. Add t remaining milk mixture, stirring constantly until blended. Remove from heat.

Pour custard into a lightly oiled 5-cu ring mold. Place mold in a large shallow pan. Pour hot water to depth of 1 inch int pan. Cover and bake at 325° for 1 hour o until a knife inserted in center of custar comes out clean.

Remove mold from water bath. Uncove and let cool on a wire rack. Cover and chi custard at least 2 hours. Loosen edges o custard with a spatula. Invert onto a serv ing plate.

Just before serving, place malted mil candies in center of ring. Serve with Ric Chocolate Sauce. Yield: 8 servings.

Rich Chocolate Sauce

¼ cup plus 2 tablespoons
   half-and-half
⅔ cup semisweet chocolate morsels
1 teaspoon vanilla extract

Bring half-and-half to a simmer in a small saucepan, stirring occasionally. Remove from heat; add chocolate morsels and vanilla, stirring until morsels melt. Let cool to room temperature. Yield: about ¾ cup.

Spring Flowers

Your home will come to life when you display one of these arrangements
that celebrates the delicate blossoms and buds of spring.

Tabletop Tulips

Use a wooden toolbox as a
unique centerpiece base
for your table. Line it with
plastic, and fill with water-
soaked oasis. Add bright
colored tulips and cover
the base with sheet moss.

Beautiful Buds

Fill the individual compo-
nents of a silver cruet set
with water, and add ranuncu-
lus. Use crystal decanters for
more than just serving spir-
its; they also make elegant
vases for additional flowers
in the grouping.

Front Door Decor

Welcome friends to your home with a front door adorned with nature's beauty. Hang a flat-backed basket on your door; line the basket with a plastic bag. Add water-soaked oasis, and insert a variety of tulips to create a fabulous pastel greeting.

Wagon Wonderland

Show off an antique German wagon by placing it in a window or in front of your fireplace. Line the wagon with plastic bags. Place a row of water-soaked oasis in the bags, and tape securely to the wagon. Cover with sheet moss, and fill with an array of spring flowers.

Oscar Night Open House

Serves 12

Popcorn   Movie Gorp

Party Pizzas

Director's Dip   Bagel Chips

Oscar's Spicy Sandwiches

Hollywood Fudge Bars

Sparkling Mineral Water

You're sure to receive the "Best Party" award when you host this gala in honor of Hollywood's finest. Set the mood by playing famous movie soundtracks as guests arrive. Nestle these movie munchies near a centerpiece of movie memorabilia including an old movie projector, movie tickets, and rolls of exposed film. Add popcorn boxes and bags overflowing with freshly popped corn. Set up director's chairs for additional seating.

Clockwise from top: Oscar's Spicy Sandwiches, Hollywood Fudge Bars, Movie Gorp, Director's Dip, bagel chips (recipes on following pages)

Party Pizzas

4 new potatoes
¼ pound thinly sliced pancetta
(Italian salt-cured bacon)
1 medium-size purple onion, sliced
3 cloves garlic, cut into thin slivers
2 (16-ounce) commercial bobolis
(see note below)
6 Roma tomatoes, thinly sliced
2 teaspoons chopped fresh rosemary
¼ cup olive oil
Arugula leaves (optional)

Cook potatoes in a small amount of boiling water 12 minutes; drain. Let cool, and slice each potato into 6 wedges.

Cook pancetta in a large skillet until crisp; remove pancetta, reserving drippings in skillet. Coarsely crumble pancetta, and set aside. Cook onion and garlic in drippings until onion is tender.

Place each boboli on a baking sheet. Top with tomato slices, onion mixture, and potato wedges. Sprinkle pancetta and rosemary over pizzas. Drizzle with olive oil.

Bake at 450° for 10 to 12 minutes. Top with arugula, if desired. Slice pizzas into thin wedges. Yield: 12 servings.

Note: Bobolis are cellophane-wrapped baked pizza crusts available in the deli section of many grocery stores.

Director's Dip

2 (6-ounce) jars marinated
artichoke hearts
1 (11-ounce) log goat cheese
4 ounces cream cheese, softened
¾ cup mayonnaise
½ cup grated Parmesan cheese,
divided
½ cup toasted, chopped pecans
2 green onions, chopped
1½ tablespoons all-purpose flour
2 teaspoons dried Italian seasoning
¾ cup soft whole wheat breadcrumbs
1 tablespoon butter or margarine,
melted
Garnish: fresh oregano sprigs, chives

Drain artichoke hearts well; chop. Combine goat cheese, cream cheese, mayonnaise, and ¼ cup Parmesan cheese in mixing bowl; beat at low speed of an electric mixer until smooth. Stir in artichokes, pecans, green onions, flour, and Italian seasoning. Spoon into an ungreased shallow 1½-quart casserole.

Combine remaining ¼ cup Parmesan cheese, breadcrumbs, and melted butter; toss gently. Sprinkle over dip.

Bake, uncovered, at 350° for 20 minutes or until dip is thoroughly heated and topping is browned. Garnish, if desired. Serve hot with bagel chips. Yield: 4½ cups.

Creative Concessions

◆ Slice Party Pizza (below) into thin wedges that will be easy to serve.

◆ Create your own invitations that resemble movie tickets, and tuck them inside popcorn boxes for delivery.

◆ Make your own "Movie Gorp" (right); just stir up your favorite mix of movie candies and granola cereal.

Oscar's Spicy Sandwiches

1 (8-ounce) package small party
    rolls on aluminum tray
⅓ cup hot red jalapeño jelly, stirred
6 (¾-ounce) slices Swiss cheese
¼ pound thinly sliced ham
2 tablespoons minced onion
2 tablespoons honey mustard
1 tablespoon brown sugar
1 tablespoon butter or margarine,
    melted
½ teaspoon curry powder
¼ teaspoon ground red pepper

Remove rolls from aluminum tray. Slice rolls in half horizontally, using a serrated knife. Return bottom halves of rolls to tray. Spread with jelly. Top with whole slices of cheese and ham. (You'll cut sandwiches apart after baking.)

Combine onion and remaining ingredients; stir well. Spread mixture over ham. Cover with tops of rolls. Cover and bake at 350° for 20 minutes or until sandwiches are thoroughly heated. To serve, cut sandwiches apart with a sharp knife. Yield: 2 dozen.

Hollywood Fudge Bars

1 cup butter or margarine
10 (1-ounce) squares semisweet
    chocolate, chopped
4 large eggs
1½ cups sugar
1 teaspoon vanilla extract
1½ cups all-purpose flour
¼ teaspoon salt
    Chocolate Frosting
    22-karat gold dust (optional)
    (see note below)

Combine butter and chocolate in top of a double boiler; bring water to a boil. Reduce heat to low; cook until butter and chocolate melt, stirring until smooth. Remove from heat, and let cool.

Beat eggs and sugar until thick and pale. Stir in melted chocolate and vanilla. Add flour and salt; mix just until blended.

Grease and flour a 13- x 9- x 2-inch pan. Pour batter into prepared pan. Bake at 350° for 28 to 30 minutes. (Do not overbake.) Let cool on a wire rack.

Frost with Chocolate Frosting. Sprinkle brownies with gold dust, if desired. Cut into bars to serve. Yield: 2 dozen.

Chocolate Frosting

¼ cup butter or margarine
2 (1-ounce) squares unsweetened
    chocolate
2½ cups sifted powdered sugar
3 to 4 tablespoons half-and-half

Combine butter and chocolate in a heavy saucepan; cook over low heat, stirring constantly, until chocolate and butter melt and mixture is smooth. Remove from heat; add powdered sugar and enough half-and-half to make mixture a good spreading consistency, stirring constantly. Yield: enough frosting for 2 dozen brownies.

Note: Edible 22-karat gold dust can be found at stores that carry cake-decorating equipment. Sifted powdered sugar may be substituted.

Games and Gifts

✦ *Provide ballots and pens for guests to predict Oscar winners.*

✦ *Suggest that each guest guess how Oscar got his name. (The statue was named by an early official of the Academy of Motion Pictures who said the statue resembled her uncle Oscar!)*

✦ *Award the winners with videotapes, celebrity-brand food items, or free movie passes.*

✦ *Send each guest home with a giant bag of flavored popcorn.*

Green Thumb
Get-Together

Serves 6

Egg Salad Crostini

Pita Niçoise

Assorted Fresh Fruit

Praline Wafers

Ruby Tea

What better way to usher in spring in all its glory than to invite friends over for a garden luncheon. The menu lends itself to several make-ahead options. The Egg Salad Crostini and Pita Niçoise filling, Praline Wafers, and Ruby Tea can all be prepared in advance. Then you'll have time to personalize each table with a unique centerpiece using a mix of garden flowers and inexpensive garden tools. Send each guest home with several gardening treasures that enhance each place setting. Short garden hoses become a conversation piece when they serve as place mats on each table. Tuck napkins inside gardening gloves and line large terra-cotta saucers with glass plates for serving the pita sandwiches and fruit.

Pita Niçoise (page 25), assorted fruit, Ruby Tea (page 26)

Garden Accents

♦ *For a unique way to serve appetizers, present Egg Salad Crostini (right) on a straw hat.*

♦ *Show off an antique wheelbarrow by using it to chill iced tea glasses before the meal begins. Line the wheelbarrow with plastic bags; fill with ice, and add glasses. Remove glasses, and fill with ice just before serving.*

Egg Salad Crostini

3 tablespoons cream cheese, softened
2 to 3 tablespoons mayonnaise
2 teaspoons honey mustard
¼ teaspoon hot sauce
3 large hard-cooked eggs, chopped
½ cup pimiento-stuffed olives, coarsely chopped
⅓ cup finely chopped celery
1 tablespoon minced onion
  Crostini
  Garnish: fresh parsley sprigs

Beat cream cheese, mayonnaise, honey mustard, and hot sauce at low speed of an electric mixer just until smooth.

Add hard-cooked eggs, olives, celery, and onion; toss gently. Cover and chill mixture thoroughly. (Egg salad mixture can be made a day ahead and kept in refrigerator.)

To serve, spoon 1 tablespoon egg salad onto each crostini. Garnish, if desired. Yield: 1 dozen appetizers.

Note: Keep any remaining egg salad mixture for guests who may prefer egg salad sandwiches instead of tuna.

Crostini

¼ French baguette
3 tablespoons butter or margarine, melted

Slice baguette into 12 thin slices (about ¼ inch thick). Brush top of each slice generously with melted butter. Place on baking sheet. Bake at 400° for 10 minutes or until crisp and golden. Let cool. Crostini may be stored in an airtight container up to 1 week. Yield: 1 dozen.

$\mathcal{P}$ita Niçoise

½ pound new potatoes
¼ pound French baby green beans
⅔ cup mayonnaise
2 large cloves garlic, crushed
1 teaspoon dried oregano
1 teaspoon lemon juice
½ teaspoon salt
½ teaspoon sugar
3 (6⅛-ounce) cans solid white tuna, drained well and chunked
1 small purple onion, finely chopped
½ cup Niçoise olives or other small black olives, sliced
2 tablespoons red wine vinegar
½ teaspoon freshly ground pepper
3 large pita bread rounds
   Red leaf lettuce
3 Roma tomatoes, thinly sliced
2 tablespoons capers (optional)

Cook potatoes in a small amount of boiling water 10 to 15 minutes or until tender. Drain; let cool to touch, and coarsely chop potatoes. Trim stem ends of beans. Arrange beans in a vegetable steamer over boiling water. Cover and steam 3 to 4 minutes or until crisp-tender. Plunge in ice water to stop cooking process; drain and cut beans into ¾-inch pieces.

Combine mayonnaise and next 5 ingredients, stirring well. Combine potatoes, beans, tuna, onion, and olives in a large bowl. Sprinkle with vinegar and pepper; toss gently. Stir in mayonnaise mixture.

Cut pita rounds in half crosswise; line each half with lettuce and tomato. Spoon tuna mixture evenly into pita halves. Sprinkle with capers, if desired. Yield: 6 servings.

Green Thumb Gifts

✦ *Guests will be delighted to receive gardening treats such as these seed packets, gardening gloves, and short garden hoses (shown below).*

✦ *Purchase cloth gloves, and paint one thumb from each pair with green latex paint.*

✦ *The small hoses are very affordable; you can find them at hardware stores.*

Pita Niçoise, fruit, Ruby Tea

Praline Wafers

⅔ cup butter
1 cup firmly packed brown sugar
1 egg yolk
1 tablespoon vanilla extract
1⅓ cups unbleached all-purpose flour
¼ teaspoon salt
⅓ cup toasted, finely chopped pecans
Pecan halves (optional)

Melt butter in a skillet. Add sugar, and cook over medium heat, stirring constantly, 3 minutes. Remove from heat, and let cool. Add egg yolk and vanilla, stirring well. Stir in flour and salt. Add chopped pecans, and stir just until blended.

Drop dough by level tablespoonfuls 2 inches apart onto ungreased cookie sheets. Press a pecan half lightly into each cookie, if desired. Bake at 375° for 8 minutes or until edges are golden. Cool 1 minute; remove to wire racks to cool completely. Yield: 3 dozen.

Ruby Tea

2 quarts cold water
1 cup sugar
4 (3-inch) sticks cinnamon, broken into pieces
1 teaspoon whole cloves
10 regular-size strawberry-flavored tea bags
4 fresh mint sprigs
1 cup pineapple juice
1 (11-ounce) bottle strawberry-flavored sparkling mineral water

Combine water, sugar, cinnamon, and cloves in a large saucepan. Bring mixture to a boil, stirring occasionally. Add tea bags and mint; remove from heat, and steep 10 minutes.

Strain tea into a pitcher. Add pineapple juice and chill thoroughly. Add sparkling water, and serve over ice. Yield: 2½ quarts.

Goodie Baskets

✦ *Double the recipe for Praline Wafers so each guest can have a goodie bag to take home.*

✦ *Wrap cookies, and place each bundle in a plastic berry basket threaded with ribbon (right). You can find plastic baskets in the produce section of your local grocery store.*

✦ *Provide a copy of the recipe for each guest.*

Gifts from the Garden

Package these simple recipes as unique gifts that show off your garden-fresh herbs and vegetables.

Red and Yellow Relish

4 sweet red peppers
3 cups fresh corn, cut from cob (about 6 ears)
2 tablespoons olive oil
2 cloves garlic, minced
4 Roma tomatoes, chopped
2 teaspoons balsamic vinegar
½ teaspoon salt
½ teaspoon ground cumin
¼ teaspoon ground red pepper

Cut peppers in half lengthwise; discard seeds and membranes. Place peppers, cut side down, on a baking sheet; flatten with palm of hand. Broil 5½ inches from heat 15 to 20 minutes or until charred. Place in a heavy-duty, zip-top plastic bag; seal and let stand 10 minutes. Peel peppers, and discard skins. Chop peppers.

Cook corn in oil in a skillet over medium-high heat 4 minutes, stirring constantly. Add garlic; cook 1 minute. Reduce heat to medium; stir in peppers, tomatoes, and remaining ingredients. Remove from heat; let cool. Store in refrigerator. Serve with grilled chicken or fish. Yield: 5 cups.

Peppered Herb Butter

1 cup unsalted butter, softened
2½ tablespoons grated Parmesan cheese
2 tablespoons chopped fresh basil
1 tablespoon chopped fresh thyme
1½ teaspoons coarsely ground pepper

Combine all ingredients in a bowl. Beat at medium speed of an electric mixer just until blended. Spoon butter mixture into miniature terra-cotta pots lined with plastic wrap. Cover and chill. Serve over grilled fish or chicken or with French bread. Yield: 1 cup.

Walnut-Basil Cheese Spread

1 (11-ounce) log goat cheese
1 (8-ounce) carton sour cream
⅔ cup toasted, chopped walnuts
½ cup finely chopped oil-packed sun-dried tomatoes, drained
½ cup minced fresh basil

Combine goat cheese and sour cream in a bowl; stir well. Stir in walnuts and remaining ingredients. Spoon into tomato shells, if desired. Cover and chill at least 2 hours. Serve at room temperature with French bread. Yield: 3 cups.

Southern Belle Baby Shower

Serves 12

Southern Spiced Nuts

Commercial Butter Mints

Vanilla-Almond Crescents

From-the-Heart Petits Fours

Pretty 'n' Pink Punch   Coffee

Honor a new belle and her mom
with a precious showcase
of tiny treasures steeped in Southern tradition.
Grace the front door with a magnolia bough
tied with pink ribbon and faux pearls.
Cover your tabletop with cherished
baby booties, bonnets, shoes, books, jewelry,
dolls, and stuffed animals.
And don't forget to polish your silver
baby cups, spoons, and picture frames.
Fill the cups with mints, and
add strands of faux pearls and pink ribbon
to trail across the table. Aromatic magnolia
blossoms and pink roses complete the theme.
And remember, all Southern
belles are known for wearing pearls.

From left: From-the-Heart Petits Fours, Vanilla-Almond
Crescents, butter mints, Southern Spiced Nuts (recipes on
following pages)

Southern Spiced Nuts

1 egg white
1 teaspoon water
1 (8-ounce) jar dry-roasted peanuts
1 cup pecan halves
¾ cup sugar
1 tablespoon pumpkin pie spice
¾ teaspoon salt

Beat egg white and water in a large bowl until foamy. Add dry-roasted peanuts and pecan halves; toss gently to coat. Combi[ne] sugar, pumpkin pie spice, and salt; add t[o] nuts, and toss until coated.

Spread mixture in a single layer in [a] lightly greased 15- x 10- x 1-inch jellyro[ll] pan. Bake at 300° for 20 minutes or unt[il] lightly browned.

Transfer immediately to wax paper. L[et] cool completely, breaking large cluste[rs] apart as they cool. Yield: 4 cups.

Vanilla-Almond Crescents

1 cup sifted powdered sugar
1 vanilla bean, split lengthwise
2½ cups all-purpose flour
1⅔ cups finely ground, toasted almonds
½ cup sifted powdered sugar
⅛ teaspoon salt
1 cup unsalted butter, cut into small pieces
2 egg yolks
2 teaspoons vanilla extract
½ teaspoon almond extract

Place 1 cup powdered sugar in a bowl. Scrape vanilla bean seeds into sugar, and stir well. Cover and set aside.

Combine flour and next 3 ingredients in a large bowl. Cut in butter with a pastry blender until mixture is crumbly. Knead in egg yolks and flavorings. Shape dough into 2-inch crescents.

Place on lightly greased cookie sheets. Bake at 325° for 15 to 18 minutes or until golden. Let cool 3 minutes on cookie sheets; dredge in reserved vanilla sugar. L[et] cool completely on wire racks. Dredge agai[n] in vanilla sugar; store in an airtight co[n]tainer. Yield: about 5 dozen.

Vanilla-Almond Crescents

From-the-Heart Petits Fours

From-the-Heart Petits Fours

2 (10¾-ounce) frozen pound cakes,
  thawed and cut into 1-inch slices
¾ cup seedless raspberry jam
½ tablespoons water
4 ounces marzipan
7 cups sifted powdered sugar
⅔ cup water, divided
¼ cup light corn syrup
1 drop of red food coloring

Cut 2 heart shapes from each slice of cake, using a 1½-inch heart-shaped cutter. Reserve excess cake for other uses.

Cook raspberry jam and 1½ tablespoons water in a small saucepan over medium-low heat, stirring until smooth. Remove from heat, and let cool slightly. Place cake hearts on a wire rack over a jellyroll pan lined with wax paper. Brush jam mixture over top and sides of cake.

Knead marzipan gently; roll between 2 sheets of plastic wrap to ¹⁄₁₆-inch thickness. Cut 28 hearts, using 1½-inch heart-shaped cutter. Place marzipan hearts over cake hearts. Cover and chill 1 hour.

Combine powdered sugar, ½ cup water, and corn syrup in a large saucepan; cook over low heat until mixture is translucent, stirring constantly. Add enough additional water, 1 tablespoon at a time, to make a good glazing consistency. Stir in red food coloring.

Spoon icing over cake hearts, coating completely. Refrigerate petits fours 15 minutes. Reheat icing over low heat, and repeat coating procedure. Yield: 28 petits fours.

Petite Sweet Hearts

◆ *Garnish your serving piece with tiny rose buds and pearls. They show off these bite-size cakes laced with raspberry and almond.*

Pretty 'n' Pink Punch

Pretty 'n' Pink Punch

⅔ cup red cinnamon candies, divided
   Vegetable cooking spray
1 quart strawberry ice cream, softened
¼ cup sugar
½ cup water
1 (46-ounce) can pineapple juice, chilled
1 (12-ounce) can frozen pink lemonade concentrate, thawed and diluted
1 (1-liter) bottle ginger ale, chilled

Sprinkle ⅓ cup candies into a 5-cup ring mold coated with cooking spray. Spoon ice cream evenly into mold. Cover and freeze until firm.

Combine remaining ⅓ cup candies, sugar, and water in a small saucepan. Bring to a boil; reduce heat, and simmer until candies dissolve, stirring occasionally. Let cool completely.

Combine syrup mixture, chilled pineapple juice, and pink lemonade in a large punch bowl; stir well. Let ice cream mold stand at room temperature 5 minutes before unmolding.

Gently stir chilled ginger ale into punch just before serving. Carefully float ice cream ring in punch. Yield: 4½ quarts.

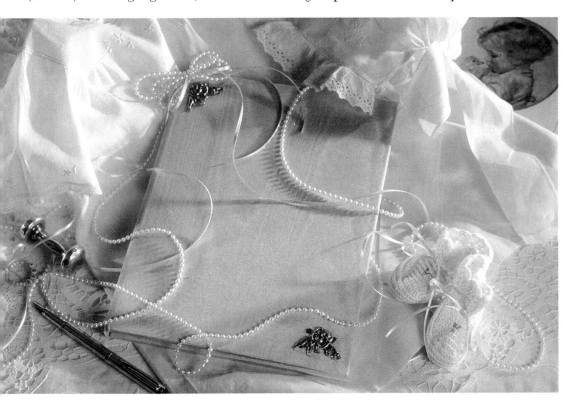

Pearls of Love

✦ *Display an ornate blank book for guests to pen "Pearls of Love" for the new baby. Present this book of sweet thoughts as a gift to the new mother.*

Party Options

Adapt this feminine theme to a Southern Gent Baby Shower by substituting little boy toys and clothes, using blue as the predominant color. Cut the petits fours into round shapes, and tint the icing blue instead of pink. Distribute bubble gum cigars as a humorous touch.

Mother's Day Breakfast in Bed

Serves 4

Sugared Bacon

Scrambled Eggs

Fresh Fruit

Mom's Muffins

Honeysuckle Cinnamon Butter

Cranapple Juice   Coffee

Awaken Mom on her special day
with a colorful tray filled with
sweet-smelling surprises—from fragrant
honeysuckle to a piping hot breakfast with
fresh brewed coffee. Snip flowers
from your garden for a simple arrangement;
drape a new pillow sham and
pillowcase across the tray table as gifts for Mom.
A special gift card announces
a new coffee mug for her collection.

On plate: Sugared Bacon, Honeysuckle Cinnamon Butter, Mom's
Muffin, fruit, scrambled eggs (recipes on following pages)

Sugared Bacon

⅓ cup firmly packed brown sugar
3 tablespoons hickory-smoked
   Worcestershire sauce
2 tablespoons spicy honey
   mustard
1 large egg, beaten
12 slices bacon
1½ cups fine, dry breadcrumbs

Combine first 4 ingredients in a shallow bowl, stirring well. Dip each slice of bacon into sugar mixture; coat with breadcrumbs. Arrange bacon slices on a rack in a large broiler pan.

Bake at 350° for 35 minutes or until bacon is crisp. Drain well on paper towels. Yield: 12 slices.

Mom's Muffins

1½ cups all-purpose flour
¾ cup sugar
½ cup honey crunch wheat germ
2 tablespoons baking powder
½ teaspoon salt
2 cups banana-nut crunch
   cereal
2 cups buttermilk
3 tablespoons roasted honey-nut
   crunchy peanut butter
3 tablespoons vegetable oil
2 large eggs, beaten
¾ cup toasted, chopped pecans

Combine first 5 ingredients in a lar
bowl; make a well in center of mixtu
Combine cereal and buttermilk; let sta

Sugar and Spice

♦ An antique fruit spoon or other serving piece is a gift that Mom will treasure for years to come.

♦ Use your personal favorite recipe for scrambled eggs. Minced fresh basil will flavor the eggs nicely, if you'd like to try a new variation.

minutes. Add peanut butter, oil, and 'gs; stir well. Add cereal mixture to dry gredients, stirring just until moistened. ently fold in pecans. Let batter stand 15 inutes.

Spoon batter into greased muffin pans, ling almost full. Bake at 400° for 20 to 5 minutes or until a wooden pick inserted center comes out clean. Remove from ns immediately, and cool on a wire rack. eld: 15 muffins.

Gifts for Mom

✦ *A new pillow sham or keepsake lace pillow (left) will enhance Mom's bedroom decor.*

✦ *Mom is bound to love a new coffee mug and a bag of flavored coffee beans to get the day off to a special start.*

Honeysuckle Cinnamon Butter

½ cup unsalted butter, softened
2 tablespoons honey
½ teaspoon ground cinnamon

Combine butter, honey, and cinnamon a small mixing bowl; beat at low speed an electric mixer 1 minute or until eamy. Cover and chill. Let stand at room mperature 20 minutes before serving. eld: ½ cup.

Party Options

Dad would appreciate breakfast in bed, too, when his day of honor rolls around in June. Why not serve a stack of hearty flapjacks with Honeysuckle Cinnamon Butter and Sugared Bacon on Father's Day? Greet Dad with a new coffee mug and the morning newspaper.

Graduation Grill

Serves 12

Bacon-Wrapped Burgers

Chunky Guacamole Salsa Catsup

Marinated New Potato Salad

Megabrownies à la Mode

Assorted Soft Drinks

ost a lively cookout for neighborhood high school graduates before they set sail for a new alma mater. A centerpiece of colored shakers will enhance school spirit. Use multicolored school boxes for serving the burgers and potato salad. Let guests dress their own burgers with guacamole, cheese, or other favorite toppings. Stack plastic flatware, napkins, and iced-down beverages in old suitcases. Take a group photo of the proud graduates, and send each one a framed copy. Present each college-bound guest with gifts such as an address book, envelopes, stamps, a corkboard with pushpins, and other school necessities. Invite the graduates to bring their high school yearbooks for signing.

Clockwise from center: Marinated New Potato Salad, Chunky Guacamole, Bacon-Wrapped Burgers (recipes on following pages)

Bacon-Wrapped Burgers

      3 pounds ground beef
     ¾ cup finely chopped onion
      2 tablespoons Greek seasoning
    24 slices bacon
    12 onion rolls
          Chunky Guacamole

Combine ground beef, onion, and Greek seasoning; shape into 12 patties.

Place 2 slices of bacon in a crisscross pattern on a flat surface. Place a patty in center of bacon; pull bacon around patty, and tie ends of bacon in a loose knot. Repeat procedure with remaining bacon and patties.

Grill hamburgers, uncovered, over medium-hot coals (350° to 400°) 6 minutes on each side or to desired degree of doneness. Serve on rolls with Chunky Guacamole, assorted cheeses, commercial salsa catsup, or other toppings. Yield: 12 servings.

Chunky Guacamole

      3 large ripe avocados, peeled
          and coarsely chopped
          (about 1 pound)
     ½ cup sour cream
      2 tablespoons mayonnaise
     ⅓ cup finely chopped
          tomato
      1 (4-ounce) can chopped green
          chiles, drained
      4 green onions, chopped
      2 tablespoons lime juice
      2 teaspoons chili powder
     ¾ teaspoon salt

Combine avocado, sour cream, and mayonnaise in a large bowl. Mash just until blended.

Add tomato and remaining ingredients; stir just until blended. Cover and chill. Yield: 4 cups.

Marinated New Potato Salad

  1½ pounds new potatoes
      1 (17-ounce) can lima beans, drained
      1 (16-ounce) can whole kernel corn,
          drained
      1 (15-ounce) can English peas,
          drained
      1 sweet red pepper, chopped
      1 medium-size purple onion, chopped
     ¾ cup sugar
     ⅓ cup white vinegar
     ¼ cup vegetable oil
     ½ teaspoon salt
     ½ teaspoon freshly ground pepper

Cook potatoes in boiling salted water to cover 15 to 18 minutes or until tender. Drain and let cool completely. Cut potatoes into quarters.

Combine potatoes, lima beans, and next 4 ingredients in a large bowl; toss gently. Combine sugar, vinegar, oil, salt, and pepper in a small saucepan; bring to a boil, stirring until sugar dissolves. Remove from heat.

Pour vinegar mixture over vegetable mixture; stir gently. Cover and chill at least 4 hours. Serve with a slotted spoon. Yield: 12 servings.

Megabrownies à la Mode

1 cup butter or margarine, softened
2½ cups sugar
4 large eggs, beaten
2 (11.75-ounce) jars hot fudge
  topping
2 cups all-purpose flour
¼ teaspoon salt
2 cups semisweet chocolate morsels
  Chocolate chip ice cream

Beat butter at medium speed of an electric mixer until soft and creamy; gradually add sugar, beating well. Add eggs, mixing well. Add fudge topping, mixing well.

Combine flour and salt; add to butter mixture, mixing just until blended. Stir in chocolate morsels. Pour batter into 2 greased and floured 9-inch square pans. Bake at 350° for 40 to 42 minutes or until a wooden pick inserted in center comes out clean. Cool completely in pans on a wire rack. Cut each pan of brownies into 6 servings; top each serving with a scoop of ice cream. Yield: 12 servings.

Party Script

✦ Provide plain T-shirts and paint pens for college-bound grads to write graffiti for each other.

✦ Encourage graduates to keep in touch with the help of their new address books.

Megabrownies à la Mode

S U M

M E R

Father's Day Courtside Cookout

Serves 6

Hickory-Smoked Kabobs

Dad's Braggin' Beans

Sweet Pineapple Coleslaw

Championship Cookies

Iced Tea   Beer

Pamper Dad on Father's Day with this sporty cookout. Serve up these juicy grilled kabobs just a few feet from the court, with the table set in honor of Dad and his love for tennis. A handsome plaid tablecloth and tennis trinkets make clever table decor. For the centerpiece, fill a thermos with gerbera daisies, and place it in a basket of new tennis balls. Indulge Dad with a new subscription to his favorite sports magazine.

Sweet Pineapple Coleslaw, Hickory-Smoked Kabobs,
Dad's Braggin' Beans (recipes on following pages)

Hickory-Smoked Kabobs

1½ pounds top sirloin steak, cut into
    1½-inch cubes
1 (8-ounce) bottle Russian salad
    dressing
¼ cup hickory-smoked
    Worcestershire sauce
1 teaspoon liquid smoke
½ teaspoon freshly ground pepper
3 small onions
12 large fresh mushrooms
1 large green pepper, cut into
    1½-inch pieces
1 large sweet red pepper, cut into
    1½-inch pieces
3 lemons, cut into wedges

Place meat in a shallow dish. Combine dressing and next 3 ingredients; stir well.

Pour mixture over meat. Cover and marinat in refrigerator 8 hours; stir occasionally.

Cook onions in boiling water to cover minutes. Drain and cut onions into quarters

Remove meat from marinade, reservin marinade. Alternate meat, onions, mush rooms, pepper pieces, and lemon wedges o six 14-inch skewers. Grill, covered, ove medium-hot coals (350° to 400°) 6 minute on each side or to desired degree of done ness, basting frequently with reserved mari nade. Squeeze lemon wedges over kabob before serving, if desired. Yield: 6 servings.

Dad's Braggin' Beans

½ pound hot ground pork sausage
1 large Vidalia onion, chopped
2 (16-ounce) cans pork and beans,
    undrained
1 (15-ounce) can black beans, drained
½ cup firmly packed dark brown
    sugar
½ cup hickory-smoked barbecue
    sauce
⅓ cup catsup
¼ cup coarse-grained mustard
¼ cup molasses
1 jalapeño pepper, minced
1 to 2 teaspoons chili powder
4 slices bacon

Brown sausage and onion in a skillet stirring until sausage crumbles. Drain Combine sausage mixture, pork and beans and next 8 ingredients in a 2½-quart casse role; stir well. Place bacon across top o beans. Bake, uncovered, at 350° for 2 hour or until desired thickness. Yield: 6 servings.

Setting the Table

✦ The meaty kabobs, spicy baked beans, and coleslaw (below) may become Dad's favorite menu.

✦ Use tennis ball cans, lids, wristbands, and sports towels as creative table decor, and add new shoestrings at Dad's place setting.

Sweet Pineapple Coleslaw

1 small cabbage (about 1½ pounds), finely shredded
2 large carrots, scraped and shredded
1 (20-ounce) can pineapple tidbits in juice, well drained
½ cup chopped purple onion
½ cup mayonnaise
⅓ cup frozen whipped topping, thawed
2 tablespoons sugar
2 tablespoons chopped fresh cilantro
½ teaspoon hot sauce
½ cup toasted, chopped pecans
Garnish: fresh cilantro sprigs

Combine shredded cabbage, carrot, pineapple tidbits, and purple onion in a large bowl. Combine mayonnaise, whipped topping, sugar, chopped cilantro, and hot sauce, stirring gently. Add to cabbage mixture; toss gently.

Cover and chill coleslaw 1 to 2 hours. Sprinkle with toasted pecans just before serving. Serve with a slotted spoon. Garnish, if desired. Yield: 6 servings.

Championship Cookies

⅔ cup butter-flavored shortening
1¼ cups firmly packed brown sugar
1 large egg
1½ cups all-purpose flour
1 teaspoon baking powder
½ teaspoon baking soda
¼ teaspoon salt
½ cup regular oats, uncooked
½ teaspoon ground cinnamon
4 (2.07-ounce) chocolate-coated caramel-peanut nougat bars, coarsely chopped
1 teaspoon vanilla extract

Beat shortening at medium speed of an electric mixer 2 minutes or until creamy; gradually add sugar, beating at medium speed 5 minutes. Add egg, beating well.

Combine flour and next 5 ingredients. Add to shortening mixture, beating at low speed just until combined. Stir in candy bars and vanilla. Chill dough 30 minutes.

Shape dough into 1½-inch balls; place 2 inches apart on ungreased cookie sheets. Bake at 350° for 8 to 10 minutes (cookies will be soft). Cool slightly on cookie sheets; remove to wire racks to cool completely. Yield: about 3 dozen.

Crowd-Pleasing Cookies

◆ Serve up a batch of Championship Cookies (above) loaded with chunky bits of candy as the grand-slam finish to Dad's special day.

◆ Present these cookies on a new tennis racquet for Dad.

Party Options

Adapt this sporty theme to a variety of occasions, such as launching a new tennis league, hosting a sports-related birthday party, having a tennis team reunion, or arranging a Wimbledon cookout. Or change the honored sport to golf, softball, or volleyball, and have a cookout in the backyard.

Easy Summer Desserts

Prepare these simple frozen desserts ahead of time. The various toppings and presentations will make them irresistible to children and adults alike.

Mile-High Frozen Strawberry Pie

Mile-High Frozen Strawberry Pie

1 (11.75-ounce) jar hot fudge topping, divided

1 (9-inch) graham cracker crumb crust

1 pint strawberry ice cream, slightly softened

5 cups vanilla ice cream

1 pint fresh strawberries, sliced

Spread ¼ cup fudge topping over bottom of crust. Spoon strawberry ice cream evenly into crust. Freeze until firm. Mound tiny scoops of vanilla ice cream over strawberry ice cream. Gently place strawberry slices between ice cream scoops. Cover and freeze pie at least 1 hour or until firm.

Place remaining fudge topping in a small saucepan. Cook over medium-low heat until thoroughly heated. Let pie stand at room temperature 5 minutes before serving; slice pie into wedges. Spoon fudge topping over each serving. Yield: one 9-inch pie.

Peanut Butter-Ice Cream Pie

6 (.8-ounce) peanut butter cup candies, frozen and chopped

1 quart vanilla ice cream, slightly softened

1 (6-ounce) chocolate-flavored crumb crust

½ (14-ounce) bag caramels

⅔ cup evaporated milk

3 tablespoons creamy peanut butter

Combine chopped peanut butter cup candies and vanilla ice cream in a large bowl; freeze until ice cream is almost firm. Spoon ice cream into chocolate flavored crumb crust, mounding up in center. Cover and freeze until firm.

Combine caramels and evaporated milk in a medium saucepan. Cook over medium-low heat, stirring constantly, until mixture is smooth.

Remove caramel sauce from heat, and stir in peanut butter. Spoon warm sauce over each serving. Yield: one 9-inch pie.

Crispy Ice Cream Sandwiches

5 cups vanilla or praline-flavored ice cream, slightly softened
4 cups miniature marshmallows
¼ cup butter or margarine
⅓ cup chunky peanut butter
6 cups crisp rice cereal

Line a 13- x 9- x 2-inch pan with heavy-duty plastic wrap, allowing 3 inches to extend over sides of pan. Spread ice cream evenly in pan. Cover and freeze until firm.

Line two 13- x 9- x 2-inch pans with aluminum foil, allowing 3 inches to extend over sides of pans. Grease foil; set aside. Combine marshmallows and butter in a large saucepan. Cook over medium heat until melted, stirring frequently.

Remove from heat, and stir in peanut butter. Working quickly, combine peanut butter mixture and cereal in a large bowl. Spread mixture into 2 prepared pans. (Mixture will be thin in pans.) Let cool completely.

Lift cereal mixture out of pans, and cut each large rectangle into 12 bars. Remove frozen ice cream from pan; cut into 12 bars. Place ice cream bars on 12 cereal bars; top with remaining 12 cereal bars, pressing gently.

Serve sandwiches immediately, or wrap in plastic wrap, and freeze until firm. Yield: 12 servings.

Double-Decker Ice Cream Pie

3 cups vanilla ice cream, slightly softened
3 (1¼-ounce) white chocolate-flavored baking bars with almonds, chopped
1 (6-ounce) chocolate-flavored crumb crust
2 cups frozen chocolate whipped topping, thawed
⅓ cup semisweet chocolate mini-morsels
Hot fudge topping

Combine ice cream and chopped candy bars; spread evenly into chocolate-flavored crumb crust. Cover and freeze 1 hour.

Combine whipped topping and chocolate mini-morsels; spread evenly over ice cream. Cover and freeze until firm.

Place fudge topping in a small saucepan. Cook over medium-low heat until thoroughly heated. Let pie stand at room temperature 5 minutes before serving. Spoon fudge topping over each serving. Yield: one 9-inch pie.

Crispy Ice Cream Sandwiches

Pint-Size Pool Party

Pucker Pops

Watermelon Fruitsicles

Strawberry Pops

Candy Ice Cream Cones

Invite the neighborhood kids over
to mark the beginning of
summer with this cool pool party. Not much
preparation is needed; just fill a small
wagon with crushed ice, and add an
assortment of frosty treats.
Children will enjoy these fruity pops wrapped
in colored plastic wrap, as they play with
pool toys and squirt guns. And, best of all,
keep any leftovers frozen for
the next summertime event.

Pucker Pops, Watermelon Fruitsicles, Strawberry Pops (page 52)

Pucker Pops

1 pint lime sherbet
1¾ cups water
½ (6-ounce) can frozen limeade
    concentrate, undiluted
24 wooden craft sticks

Combine first 3 ingredients in container of an electric blender; process until smooth. Pour mixture into ice cube trays; freeze 30 minutes or until almost firm. Insert a wooden stick into center of each cube; freeze until firm. Remove from trays, and wrap in heavy-duty plastic wrap. Store in freezer. Yield: 2 dozen.

Watermelon Fruitsicles

1 (5-pound) watermelon wedge,
    seeded and cubed
½ cup sugar
1 envelope unflavored gelatin
1 tablespoon lemon juice

Place half of watermelon in container of an electric blender; process until smooth. Repeat procedure with remaining watermelon. Strain watermelon puree into a large measuring cup, discarding pulp. Reserve 4 cups watermelon juice.

Combine 1 cup juice and sugar in a saucepan. Sprinkle gelatin over mixture; let stand 1 minute. Cook over medium heat, stirring constantly, until sugar and gelatin dissolve. Add gelatin mixture to remaining 3 cups watermelon juice; stir in lemon juice, and let cool. Pour into ⅓-cup frozen pop molds; freeze. Yield: 1 dozen.

Strawberry Pops

2 cups strawberry frozen yogurt
1 (10-ounce) package frozen
    strawberries in light syrup,
    thawed and undrained
½ (12-ounce) can frozen pink
    lemonade, undiluted
12 (3-ounce) paper cups
12 wooden craft sticks

Combine first 3 ingredients in container of an electric blender; process until smooth. Pour evenly into paper cups. Cover top of cups with aluminum foil, and insert wooden stick through foil into center of each cup. Freeze until firm. To serve, remove foil, and peel paper cup away from each Strawberry Pop. Yield: 1 dozen.

Candy Ice Cream Cones

1 (14-ounce) can sweetened
    condensed milk
⅔ cup chocolate syrup
⅓ cup semisweet chocolate morsels
    or peanut butter morsels
⅓ cup chopped cream-filled
    chocolate sandwich cookies
⅓ cup chopped peanut butter cup
    candies
⅓ cup chopped English
    toffee-flavored candy bars or
    other desired candy bars
2 cups whipping cream
18 ice cream cones

Combine sweetened condensed milk and chocolate syrup in a large bowl; stir well.

Stir in chocolate or peanut butter morsels, chocolate sandwich cookies, and chopped candies.

Beat whipping cream at high speed of an electric mixer until soft peaks form. Gradually fold whipped cream into candy mixture. Cover and freeze until firm.

To serve, scoop ice cream and place on cones. Yield: 1½ dozen.

Variation: To make **Ice Cream on a Stick**, spoon candy mixture (above) into muffin pans lined with foil baking cups. Freeze cups 30 minutes or until almost firm. Insert a wooden craft stick into center of each cup, and freeze until firm. To serve, peel off foil baking cups.

Chilling Out

✦ *An acrylic ice cream cone holder shows off this candy-filled concoction that children will devour in minutes.*

Candy Ice Cream Cones

New Neighbors' Breakfast in a Box

Chocolate-Zucchini Gems

Blueberry Crunch Loaf

Gingersnap Pancake Mix

Welcome your new neighbors to town with this goodie box full of quick breads, pancake mix, syrup, coffee, and preserves. Be sure to include maps and brochures suggesting things to do around the city. Package the Chocolate-Zucchini Gems and Blueberry Crunch Loaf in cellophane bags. Seal the pancake mix in a zip-top plastic bag; then place it in a fabric bag. And for a special touch, label each food gift with a doily tag. Personalize a wooden Shaker box with stenciling, and glue ribbon around edges of the box and lid. As an alternative, fill a decorative hat box or large basket with these same breakfast gifts.

Left to right: Box with packaged Chocolate-Zucchini Gems and Gingersnap Pancake Mix, Blueberry Crunch Loaf (recipes on following pages)

Chocolate-Zucchini Gems

½ cup butter or margarine, softened
1 cup sugar
2 large eggs
⅔ cup sour cream
1 teaspoon baking soda
1⅓ cups all-purpose flour
3 tablespoons unsweetened cocoa
¼ teaspoon salt
¾ cup shredded zucchini
⅓ cup semisweet chocolate
    mini-morsels
1 teaspoon vanilla extract

Beat butter at medium speed of an electric mixer until creamy; gradually add sugar, beating until light and fluffy. Add eggs, one at a time, beating well after each addition.

Combine sour cream and soda; let stand 5 minutes. Combine flour, cocoa, and salt; add to creamed mixture alternately with sour cream mixture, beginning and ending with flour mixture. Mix after each addition. Stir in zucchini, mini-morsels, and vanilla.

Place paper baking cups in miniature (1¾-inch) muffin pans. Spoon batter into paper cups, filling two-thirds full. Bake at 400° for 10 minutes or until a wooden pick inserted in center comes out clean. Remove from pans, and cool on wire racks. Yield: about 5 dozen.

Blueberry Crunch Loaf

¼ cup butter or margarine, softened
1 (3-ounce) package cream cheese, softened
1 cup sugar
2 large eggs
2 cups all-purpose flour
2 teaspoons baking powder
¼ teaspoon baking soda
¼ teaspoon salt
⅓ cup milk
1 cup fresh or frozen blueberries (see note below)
3 tablespoons brown sugar
2 tablespoons regular oats, uncooked
2 tablespoons chopped pecans
1 tablespoon all-purpose flour
1 tablespoon butter or margarine, melted

Beat ¼ cup butter and cream cheese at medium speed of an electric mixer 2 minutes or until creamy. Gradually add 1 cup sugar, beating at medium speed 5 minutes. Add eggs, one at a time, beating after each addition.

Combine 2 cups flour, baking powder, soda, and salt. Add to butter mixture alternately with milk, beginning and ending with flour mixture. Gently fold in blueberries. Spoon batter into a greased and floured 9- x 5- x 3-inch loafpan.

Combine brown sugar and remaining ingredients in a small bowl; stir just until combined. Sprinkle streusel mixture over batter. Bake at 350° for 1 hour or until a wooden pick inserted in center comes out clean. Cool in pan on a wire rack 15 minutes. Remove from pan, and let cool completely on wire rack. Yield: one 9-inch loaf.

Note: If using frozen blueberries, pat dry on paper towels; toss with 2 tablespoons all-purpose flour before stirring into batter.

Gingersnap Pancake Mix

- 3 cups all-purpose flour
- ¼ cup baking powder
- 2 teaspoons salt
- 3 cups crushed gingersnap cookies (about 60 cookies)
- 1 cup instant nonfat dry milk powder
- ½ cup sugar
- 2 tablespoons ground ginger
- ¾ cup butter-flavored shortening

Combine first 7 ingredients in a large bowl, stirring well. Cut in shortening with a pastry blender until mixture is crumbly.

Place pancake mix in an airtight container, and store in a cool dry place up to 6 weeks. Yield: 9 cups.

Gingersnap Pancakes

- 1 cup Gingersnap Pancake Mix
- 1 large egg, lightly beaten
- ½ cup milk

Place pancake mix in a small bowl, and make a well in center. Combine egg and milk, stirring well. Add milk mixture to pancake mix, stirring just until dry ingredients are moistened.

Preheat griddle to 325°; lightly grease griddle. For each pancake, pour ¼ cup batter onto hot griddle. Cook pancakes until tops are covered with bubbles and edges look cooked; turn and cook other side. Serve with whipped butter and molasses, syrup, apple butter, or powdered sugar. Yield: 6 (4-inch) pancakes.

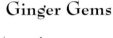

Ginger Gems

◆ *When giving Gingersnap Pancake Mix as a gift, be sure to include a handwritten recipe card for Gingersnap Pancakes (left).*

◆ *Complement the spicy ginger flavor of the pancakes with a topping of syrup, molasses, or apple butter.*

Great Gift Baskets

These bountiful gift baskets will express sentiments to suit a wide variety of occasions, including birthdays and weddings.

Tea-Lover's Treasure

It's easy to transform an inexpensive wicker tray into a special gift basket filled with goodies that would tickle a tea-lover's fancy. Include a variety of loose tea, assorted tea bags, a tea infuser spoon, decorative tea balls, and a book about teas. Add a plate full of freshly baked scones and a matching teacup and saucer. (You can find cups and saucers at tag sales or antique stores.) Tie the tray with tulle, and add a small gift tag, ribbon, and a sprig of dried flowers.

Honeymoon Getaway

Present a picnic basket full of blessings to a newlywed couple as they make their getaway. Fill it with a sampling of foods from their reception, a bottle of champagne with two flutes tied together, a disposable camera with film, bubble bath, suntan lotion, candles, and inexpensive sunglasses. And be sure to include a "Do Not Disturb" sign.

Herb Gardener's Delight

Here's a basket that's sure to delight any gardener. Fill an English trug, another type of gathering basket, or a watering can with essentials for an herb garden. Use Spanish moss as filler, and add a bag of potting soil, packaged dried herbs, seed packets, garden tools, gloves, and decorative small terra-cotta pots. Finish the collection with a bottle of herb oil or herb vinegar.

Fourth of July Beach Party

Serves 8

Shrimp Cocktail in Shells

Catch-of-the-Day Hoagies with Red Onion Relish

Potato Chips

Piña Colada Ice Cream

Shortbread Shells

Beer   Wine Coolers   Soft Drinks

One of the most festive places to celebrate Independence Day is at the beach with family and friends. Set up the meal right down by the water's edge so you can enjoy a beautiful sunset. Decorate a portable table with sand pails and beach toys filled with sand and shells. Add sparklers to turn the event into a dazzling celebration. Ice down a variety of drinks in a durable plastic tub. Bake the Shortbread Shell cookies in advance. Churn the ice cream, and let it ripen while the catch-of-the-day sizzles on the grill. Light the sparklers after dinner, and enjoy the patriotic festivities.

Catch-of-the-Day Hoagies with Red Onion Relish (page 63)   61

Shrimp Cocktail in Shells

Seashells, cleaned and dried
2 quarts water
3 pounds unpeeled large fresh shrimp
1½ cups commercial cocktail sauce
1½ tablespoons prepared horseradish

Place a medium-size glass bowl in a large glass bowl. Pour boiling water between 2 bowls until water comes to ½ inch below rims. Tape rims of bowls together with masking tape. Position seashells down in water between bowls. Freeze 8 hours.

Bring 2 quarts water to a boil; add shrimp, and cook 3 to 5 minutes. Drain; rinse with cold water. Chill. Peel and devei shrimp, leaving tails intact. Combine cock tail sauce and horseradish, stirring well.

Remove shell bowl from freezer. Pour co water into medium bowl. Dip large outer bow into cold water. (Do not use warm water ice may crack.) Use a kitchen towel to gentl remove frozen shell bowl from glass bowls.

Place shrimp in frozen shell bowl; set she bowl in a flat basket or grapevine wreath line with a plastic bag. (Fill basket with ice, desired.) Serve with cocktail sauce and lemo wedges, if desired. Serve immediately. Yield: appetizer servings.

Shrimp in Shells

◆ Use shells that you collect along the beach for this unique icy serving bowl (above and right).

◆ Spoon the cocktail sauce into large seashells.

◆ Provide decorative wooden picks for dipping shrimp in cocktail sauce.

Catch-of-the-Day Hoagies
With Red Onion Relish

½ pounds grouper, amberjack, red
    snapper, or other firm-fleshed
    fish fillet
¾ cup red wine vinegar
¼ cup olive oil
1 tablespoon brown sugar
2 tablespoons honey mustard
4 cloves garlic, minced
½ teaspoon freshly ground
    pepper
8 (6- to 7-inch) French bread
    loaves, split lengthwise
⅓ cup olive oil
    Fresh Herb Mayonnaise
    Red leaf lettuce
    Red Onion Relish

Cut fish into 8 serving-size pieces, and
place in a shallow dish. Combine vinegar
and next 5 ingredients, stirring well. Pour
mixture over fish. Cover and marinate in
refrigerator 1 hour.

Remove fish from marinade, discarding
marinade. Grill fish, covered, over medium
coals (300° to 350°) 6 to 8 minutes on
each side or until fish flakes easily when
tested with a fork.

Brush cut sides of French bread loaves
with ⅓ cup olive oil. Grill bread, cut sides
down, covered, over medium coals 3 to 4
minutes or until toasted. Remove bread
from grill, and wrap in aluminum foil. Keep
warm until just before serving.

To serve, spread Fresh Herb Mayonnaise
evenly on bottom of each French bread loaf.
Place lettuce, grilled fish, and Red Onion
Relish on bottom halves; replace tops. Yield:
8 servings.

Fresh Herb Mayonnaise

1 cup mayonnaise
1 tablespoon chopped fresh basil
1 tablespoon chopped fresh oregano
1 tablespoon chopped fresh thyme
1 large clove garlic, crushed

Combine all ingredients in a small bowl,
stirring well. Cover and chill at least 1 hour.
Yield: 1 cup.

Red Onion Relish

2 pounds purple onions, sliced
¼ cup butter or margarine, melted
½ cup balsamic vinegar
3 tablespoons brown sugar
½ teaspoon freshly ground pepper

Cook onions in butter in a Dutch oven
over medium heat 15 minutes or until very
tender, stirring occasionally. Add vinegar,
brown sugar, and pepper. Cook, uncovered,
over medium heat 12 to 14 minutes or
until liquid is absorbed, stirring occasionally. Remove from heat, and let cool to room
temperature. Yield: 1½ cups.

Surfside Sandwich

◆ *American flag
picks help carry
out the patriotic
theme for this
handsome coastal
sandwich.*

Piña Colada Ice Cream, Shortbread She[...]

Piña Colada Ice Cream

1 quart milk
½ cups sugar
1 cup cream of coconut
5 egg yolks, lightly beaten
1 quart half-and-half
½ cup flaked coconut
¼ cup light rum
1 (15¼-ounce) can crushed
   pineapple in heavy syrup, drained

Combine first 3 ingredients in a large saucepan. Cook over medium heat, stirring constantly, until sugar dissolves. Gradually stir about one-fourth of hot milk mixture into yolks; add to remaining hot mixture, stirring constantly. Cook over medium heat, stirring constantly, 2 to 3 minutes or until thermometer reaches 160°. Remove from heat; let cool. Stir in half-and-half, flaked coconut, and rum. Cover and chill custard thoroughly.

Pour custard into freezer container of a 5-quart hand-turned or electric freezer. Freeze according to manufacturer's instructions. Remove dasher, and stir in crushed pineapple. Cover and pack freezer with additional ice and rock salt; let stand 1 hour before serving. Yield: about 1 gallon.

Shortbread Shells

⅔ cup butter, softened
¾ cup sifted powdered sugar
½ teaspoons coconut extract
1 teaspoon vanilla extract
¼ cups all-purpose flour
¼ teaspoon salt
   Vegetable cooking spray

Beat butter at medium speed of an electric mixer until creamy. Gradually add sugar, beating until light and fluffy. Add flavorings; beat well. Gradually stir in flour and salt.

Place 1 tablespoon of dough onto outside of each 2½-inch-wide scallop baking shell coated with cooking spray. Gently press dough over each shell, leaving ⅛-inch border around shell to allow for expansion during baking.

Place shells, dough side up, on ungreased cookie sheets. Bake at 325° for 20 to 22 minutes or until lightly browned. Let cool completely on wire racks; carefully remove cookies from shells. Store cookies in an airtight container up to 1 week. Yield: 28 cookies.

Great Garnishes

◆ *Shortbread Shells (left) carry out the seashell theme as dippers for Piña Colada Ice Cream.*

◆ *Tiny straw hats with red, white, and blue ribbon suspended from wooden picks make a playful garnish.*

An Engaging Evening

Serves 16

Fruit and Cheese Tray

Crackers   Shrimp Butter   Bread

Savory Palmiers

White Wine

Caramel-Brownie Cheesecake

Strawberry Flowers

Coffee   Champagne

ere's a "novel" idea for an engagement party—host a book shower to which guests bring book-related gifts for the honored couple. Purchase small antique books to send as invitations. Into each book, insert a page of parchment paper printed with party details; mark the page with ribbon. Feature unique book themes and foods in various rooms of your home. For example, display gardening books on the patio and antique volumes in the library. Use the same approach with food—serve savory snacks with wine in the library or kitchen, and end the festivities with dessert, coffee, and champagne on the patio.

Caramel-Brownie Cheesecake,
Strawberry Flowers (recipes on page 71)

Announcing
a
"New Chapter"
In the lives of
Kath and Phil

Please join us as we
Celebrate
Their Story
Saturday
July 18th
7:00pm
103 Oxford Cove
Please bring a book related gift!

Shrimp Butter

1½ pounds frozen tiny cooked
      shrimp, thawed and
      drained
½ cup butter, softened
1 (8-ounce) container cream cheese
      with chives, softened
¼ cup chopped onion
¼ cup mayonnaise
1 tablespoon prepared
      horseradish
2 cloves garlic, halved
2 teaspoons cocktail sauce
½ teaspoon hot sauce
¼ teaspoon salt
      Garnish: 1 small cooked
      shrimp (optional)

Position knife blade in food processor
bowl; add 1½ pounds cooked shrimp, butter, and cream cheese with chives. Cover
and process until smooth, scraping down
sides of bowl occasionally.

Add onion, mayonnaise, horseradish,
garlic, cocktail sauce, hot sauce, and salt;
pulse just until mixture is blended.

Transfer mixture to a small serving container; cover and chill thoroughly. Let butter stand at room temperature 15 minutes
before serving.

Serve Shrimp Butter with assorted
crackers, or spread on party rye bread or
pumpernickel bread. Garnish, if desired.
Yield: 4 cups.

$\mathcal{S}$avory Palmiers

1 (17¼-ounce) package frozen puff
   pastry, thawed
1 (4.25-ounce) jar champagne
   mustard, divided
1 cup grated Parmesan cheese
1½ tablespoons dried oregano
2 teaspoons garlic powder
8 ounces thinly sliced prosciutto ham
1 large egg, lightly beaten

Place 1 pastry sheet on a work surface; spread half of mustard evenly over pastry. Combine cheese, oregano, and garlic powder; sprinkle half of cheese mixture over mustard. Arrange half of prosciutto slices evenly over cheese mixture. Lightly press prosciutto into cheese. Roll up pastry, jellyroll fashion, starting at 1 side and ending at middle of pastry sheet.

Roll up other side of pastry, jellyroll fashion, until both rolls meet in the middle. Cover and chill roll at least 30 minutes. Repeat procedure with remaining pastry sheet, mustard, cheese mixture, and ham.

Cut rolls crosswise into ½-inch-thick slices. (Slices will resemble a figure "8.") Place slices on lightly greased baking sheets. Brush top of each palmier with beaten egg.

Bake at 350° for 25 minutes or until puffed and golden. Serve warm or at room temperature. Yield: about 3½ dozen.

Bachelor's Bounty

◆ Create a bachelor's handsome library setting for serving Shrimp Butter, Savory Palmiers, and a fruit and cheese platter (left).

◆ Let theme-related gifts such as ornate bookends, an antique miniature book collection, and a reading lamp add to the display. A pair of antique reading glasses, some classic novels, and a bottle of white wine complete the scene.

Strawberry Flower
Caramel-Brownie Cheesecake

Caramel-Brownie Cheesecake

1¾ cups vanilla wafer crumbs
¼ cup plus 1 tablespoon butter or
    margarine, melted
1 (14-ounce) package caramels
1 (5-ounce) can evaporated milk
2 cups coarsely crumbled unfrosted
    brownies (see note below)
3 (8-ounce) packages cream cheese,
    softened
1 cup firmly packed brown sugar
3 large eggs
1 (8-ounce) carton sour cream
2 teaspoons vanilla extract
    Garnishes: whipped cream,
    chocolate-lined wafer roll cookies

Combine vanilla wafer crumbs and butter, stirring well. Press mixture firmly in bottom and 2 inches up sides of a 9-inch springform pan. Bake at 350° for 5 minutes. Let cool completely on a wire rack.

Combine caramels and milk in a small heavy saucepan; cook over low heat, stirring often, until caramels melt. Pour caramel mixture over crust. Sprinkle crumbled brownies over caramel.

Beat cream cheese at medium speed of an electric mixer 2 minutes or until light and fluffy. Gradually add sugar, mixing well. Add eggs, one at a time, beating just until blended. Stir in sour cream and vanilla.

Pour batter into prepared crust. Bake at 350° for 50 to 60 minutes or until cheesecake is almost set. Remove from oven, and let cool to room temperature on a wire rack. Cover and chill at least 4 hours.

Remove sides of springform pan; garnish, if desired. Yield: one 9-inch cheesecake.

Note: Buy prepackaged unfrosted brownies from a bakery, or prepare your favorite mix; let cool and crumble enough to yield 2 cups.

Strawberry Flowers

32 medium strawberries
1 (8-ounce) package cream cheese,
    softened
1 (3-ounce) package cream cheese,
    softened
3 tablespoons powdered sugar
¼ teaspoon almond extract
2 tablespoons grated semisweet
    chocolate

Cut a thin slice from the stem end of each strawberry, allowing the berries to stand upright. Place berries, cut side down, on a serving platter. Cut each berry into 4 wedges, cutting to, but not through, bottoms. Fan wedges slightly; set aside.

Combine cream cheese, sugar, and almond extract in a mixing bowl. Beat at medium speed of an electric mixer until light and fluffy. Fold in grated chocolate. Spoon mixture into a decorating bag fitted with a large star tip. Pipe cream cheese mixture into center of each berry. Chill until ready to serve. Yield: 32 strawberry flowers.

Novel Gifts

◆ *Gift books about travel, art, gardening, cooking, romance, and poetry fit the party's theme.*

◆ *Other ideas include (far left) a photo album, letter opener, blank book, journal, diary, address book, bookstand, and magnifying glass.*

A Lazy
Labor Day

Serves 8

Almond and Herb-Crusted Trout

Crispy Skewered Potatoes

Grilled Tomato Fans

Cookies 'n' Cream Peach Cobbler

Iced Tea   Soft Drinks   Beer

Reel in your fishing buddies for
this casual gathering to mark
the nearing of summer's end. Pack up your
fishing gear, and head to a shady riverbank or a
peaceful lake. Grab a fishing creel to transport
plates, flatware, cups, and napkins, and
let a cricket box double as a vase for wildflowers.
The menu makes the most of the
end of summer's bounty, using fresh peaches
and ripe tomatoes. And, of course, the
main attraction for the anglers in the crowd
is hooking the freshwater trout.

Grilled Tomato Fans, Almond and Herb-Crusted
Trout, Crispy Skewered Potatoes (recipes on following pages)

Almond and Herb-Crusted Trout

2/3 cup saltine cracker crumbs
1/3 cup ground almonds
3 tablespoons chopped fresh thyme
1/2 teaspoon pepper
2 pounds trout fillets
1/2 cup milk
2/3 cup vegetable oil
Garnish: fresh thyme sprigs

Combine cracker crumbs, groun[d] almonds, 3 tablespoons chopped thyme, an[d] pepper in a shallow bowl; stir well. Dip trou[t] fillets in milk. Dredge fillets in crack[er] crumb mixture.

Panfry fillets, a few at a time, in hot oi[l] in a large heavy skillet 3 minutes on eac[h] side or until golden. Drain on paper towel[s]. Garnish, if desired. Yield: 8 servings.

Trout by the Brook

✦ *An almond and cracker crumb topping gives these trout fillets a crisp coating. The skewered pota-toes and tomato fans require minimal prep-aration; place them on the grill briefly for browning and melting cheese.*

Crispy Skewered Potatoes

20 new potatoes
3 tablespoons orange marmalade
2 tablespoons butter or margarine, melted
1 teaspoon brown sugar
1 teaspoon grated orange rind
½ teaspoon pepper
Salt

Cook potatoes, covered, in boiling water to cover just until crisp-tender (about 12 minutes). Drain and let cool. Cut potatoes in half. Thread potatoes onto skewers.

Combine marmalade and next 4 ingredients, stirring well. Brush marmalade mixture over potatoes.

Grill, covered, over medium-hot coals (350° to 400°) 8 minutes or until potatoes are browned, turning after 4 minutes, and basting with any remaining marmalade mixture. Sprinkle potatoes with salt before serving. Yield: 8 servings.

Grilled Tomato Fans

8 medium-size firm, ripe tomatoes
2 (6-ounce) packages sliced mozzarella cheese
24 large fresh basil leaves
⅓ cup extra-virgin olive oil
3 large cloves garlic, crushed
2 tablespoons chopped fresh thyme
¾ teaspoon dried crushed red pepper

Turn each tomato on its side. Cut 3 vertical slits in each tomato, cutting almost to, but not through, bottom. Cut each slice of cheese crosswise into 6 equal pieces. Place 2 pieces of cheese and a basil leaf in each slit.

Place each tomato in the center of a large square of heavy-duty aluminum foil. Combine oil and remaining ingredients; drizzle oil mixture evenly over tomatoes. Fold foil securely around each tomato.

Grill, covered, over medium-hot coals (350° to 400°) 8 to 10 minutes or until tomatoes are heated and cheese melts. Unwrap and transfer tomatoes to a serving platter. Serve immediately. Yield: 8 servings.

Cookies 'n' Cream Peach Cobbler

Cookies 'n' Cream Peach Cobbler

¾ cup sugar
½ tablespoons cornstarch
½ teaspoon ground cinnamon
¼ cup amaretto (optional)
¼ cup peach preserves
10 large ripe peaches (about 3 pounds), peeled and sliced
⅓ (20-ounce) package refrigerated sliceable sugar cookie dough
1 tablespoon all-purpose flour, divided
½ tablespoons sugar
¼ teaspoon ground cinnamon
    Vanilla ice cream

Combine first 3 ingredients in a large saucepan; stir well. Stir in amaretto, if desired, and peach preserves. Add sliced peaches, and stir gently to coat.

Cook over medium heat, stirring frequently, until mixture is thickened and bubbly. Spoon peach mixture into a lightly greased 11- x 7- x 1½-inch baking dish.

Place cookie dough between 2 sheets of plastic wrap on a cookie sheet; roll to a 10- x 7-inch rectangle. Remove top sheet of plastic wrap, and sprinkle dough with 1½ teaspoons flour; gently rub flour into dough. Repeat procedure on other side of dough. Freeze dough 15 minutes.

Cut 6 (10- x ½-inch) strips of dough, using a pastry wheel. Cut 8 (6- x ½-inch) strips of dough. Arrange strips in lattice design over peach mixture in dish. Combine 1½ tablespoons sugar and ¼ teaspoon cinnamon. Sprinkle over cookie dough.

Bake at 350° for 30 to 35 minutes or until golden brown. Let cobbler cool 15 minutes on a wire rack. Spoon into individual serving bowls, and top with ice cream. Yield: 8 servings.

Note: Slice and bake remaining cookie dough according to package directions. Serve additional cookies with cobbler and ice cream, if desired.

A Peachy Pastime

◆ *Present a freshly baked peach cobbler (far left) with its sugar cookie crust on a fisherman's stool.*

◆ *Keep a basket of fresh peaches nearby for late afternoon snacking while waiting for more fish to bite.*

◆ *For a no-fuss tablecloth, cover your picnic table in newspaper; call it "fishing linens."*

◆ *Ice down drinks in a clean minnow bucket.*

New Orleans Supper Club

Serves 8

Muffuletta Canapés

Beer

Salad Greens with Nasturtiums

Gumbo Pot Pies

Red Wine   Water

Bananas Foster Parfaits

Coffee

Jazz up your supper club with Louisiana lagniappe (a little something extra). Welcome guests to the sights and sounds of old New Orleans recreated on your patio. Turn on soft jazz music just before guests arrive. Dress up your courtyard with lush ferns, caladiums, garden statuaries, sculptures, and urns. Use a cherub statuary as the centerpiece base to hold a plant or flowers. Begin the meal with muffuletta appetizers and cold beer that's been chilling in a pedestal birdbath filled with ice.

Gumbo Pot Pies (page 81)

◆ *Serve this attractive salad in a large urn lined with a plastic bowl. A miniature wrought iron bench adds to the themed decor. You can find miniature iron treasures at antique shops.*

◆ *If nasturtiums are unavailable for your salad, substitute other edible flowers like pansies or snapdragons.*

Muffuletta Canapés

1 (12-ounce) jar pickled mixed
    vegetables, drained well
¼ cup pimiento-stuffed olive slices,
    chopped
2 ounces thinly sliced salami, finely
    chopped
1 tablespoon minced garlic
1 tablespoon olive oil
2 (10-ounce) cans refrigerated flaky
    biscuits
½ cup finely shredded provolone
    cheese

Finely chop mixed vegetables. Combine vegetables, olives, salami, garlic, and olive oil. Cover and chill at least 1 hour.

Bake biscuits according to package directions. Let cool slightly. Using a melon baller or small spoon, carefully scoop out center of 16 biscuits. (Reserve remaining biscuits for another use.)

Stir cheese into olive salad mixture. Spoon 1 heaping tablespoon olive salad into each hollowed-out biscuit. Bake at 400° fo 8 to 10 minutes or until thoroughly hea ed. Serve warm. Yield: 16 appetizers.

Salad Greens With Nasturtiums

12 cups torn assorted salad greens
⅓ cup olive oil or walnut oil
3 tablespoons balsamic vinegar
1 shallot, minced
1 tablespoon water
1½ tablespoons raspberry mustard
1 teaspoon sugar
½ teaspoon salt
½ teaspoon freshly ground pepper
  Edible nasturtiums

Combine salad greens in a salad bow toss gently. Combine oil and next 7 ingr dients; stir well. Drizzle dressing mixtu over salad greens. Top with nasturtium Yield: 8 servings.

Gumbo Pot Pies

1 (2½-pound) broiler-fryer
2 quarts water
1 onion, quartered
2 bay leaves
½ cup all-purpose flour
½ cup vegetable oil
1 large green pepper, chopped
1 large onion, chopped
3 cloves garlic, chopped
2 pounds fresh or frozen okra, cut
    in ¾-inch slices
2 (10-ounce) cans whole tomatoes
    and green chiles
1 pound andouille sausage, sliced
1 tablespoon dried thyme
1 pound unpeeled large fresh shrimp
2 (17¼-ounce) packages frozen
    puff pastry, thawed
1 large egg, lightly beaten

Combine broiler-fryer, water, quartered onion, and bay leaves in a Dutch oven. Bring to a boil. Cover, reduce heat, and simmer 1 hour or until chicken is tender.

Remove chicken; reserve 1½ cups broth, and discard onion and bay leaves. Let chicken cool. Skin, bone, and coarsely chop chicken.

Combine flour and oil in Dutch oven. Cook over medium heat, stirring constantly, 15 to 20 minutes or until roux is chocolate colored. Add green pepper, chopped onion, and garlic; sauté 2 minutes. Add okra, tomatoes and green chiles, sausage, thyme, and reserved 1½ cups broth. Cover and simmer 30 minutes.

Peel and devein shrimp; stir shrimp and chicken into gumbo. Cook just until shrimp turn pink. Remove from heat, and set aside to cool slightly.

Roll each pastry sheet out on a floured surface. Cut 4 circles out of each sheet of pastry, ½-inch larger than rims of individual 2-cup soup crocks. Return pastry to freezer for at least 15 minutes. Cut out decorative leaf shapes from excess pastry strips.

Ladle gumbo into crocks, filling three-fourths full. Brush top edges of pastry circles with beaten egg. Invert and place 1 pastry circle over each bowl, pressing firmly to sides of bowl to seal edges. Apply decorative leaves on top of pastry. Brush top of each pastry circle and leaves with beaten egg. Bake pot pies at 400° for 20 minutes or until pastry is puffed and golden. Yield: 8 servings.

Lagniappe

◆ *Use miniature instrument ornaments as napkin rings; send them home with guests as favors. (Plastic Christmas ornaments are just the right size.)*

◆ *Miniature urns and popular jazz tapes also make special party favors for guests.*

Bananas Foster Parfaits

1 cup sugar
1 (5.1-ounce) package vanilla
   instant pudding mix
3 cups evaporated milk, chilled
½ cup whipping cream, whipped
5 large bananas, sliced
⅓ cup firmly packed dark brown
   sugar
2 tablespoons butter or margarine
⅓ cup dark rum
¼ cup crème de banana liqueur
1 (10¾-ounce) frozen pound cake,
   thawed and cut into 1-inch cubes
½ cup whipping cream
1 tablespoon powdered sugar

Place 1 cup sugar in a heavy skillet. Cook over medium heat, stirring with a wooden spoon, until sugar melts and turns golden (about 10 minutes). Pour mixture quickly into a jellyroll pan lined with aluminum foil; let cool. Break candy into coarse pieces.

Prepare pudding mix according to package directions, but using 3 cups evaporated milk. Fold whipped cream into pudding.

Cook bananas in brown sugar and butter in a large skillet over medium heat just until sugar melts and bananas are glazed. Remove from heat, and stir in rum.

Sprinkle banana liqueur evenly over pound cake cubes. Layer pudding, cake cubes, glazed bananas, and remaining pudding in 8 large glasses.

Beat ½ cup whipping cream until foamy; gradually add powdered sugar, beating until soft peaks form. Dollop whipped cream over parfaits. Top with candy. Yield: 8 servings.

Bananas Foster Parfaits

UMN

Texas Tailgating

Serves 8

Cowboy Boots with a Kick

Southwestern Salsa   Tortilla Chips

Sizzling Barbecue Sandwiches

Vegetable Sticks

Yellow Rose Pound Cake

Soft Drinks   Beer

apture the spirit of the Lone Star State with this menu that comes deep from the heart of Texas. Round up a scenic view and drape a southwestern blanket from the tailgate to set the mood. Mix the rustic beauty of authentic western gear with this spicy menu to experience a taste of Texas chic. For starters, guests will enjoy sampling cactus as the secret ingredient that distinguishes this piquant salsa. Serve the jumbo sandwiches from spatterpainted graniteware plates, and lasso the flatware in small burlap napkins. To display the famous yellow rose of Texas, use western boots as vases, tucking a small glass in each boot to hold the flowers and water.

From left: Vegetable sticks, tortilla chips, Sizzling Barbecue Sandwiches, Southwestern Salsa and more chips (recipes on following pages)

Cowboy Boots
With a Kick

1½ cups all-purpose flour
1 teaspoon dried crushed red pepper
½ teaspoon garlic powder
½ teaspoon chili powder
⅔ cup butter, cut up
1½ cups (6 ounces) finely shredded
    Colby Jack cheese
2 tablespoons cold water

Combine first 4 ingredients in a bowl; cut in butter with a pastry blender until mixture is crumbly. Stir in cheese. Sprinkle cold water, 1 tablespoon at a time, evenly over surface; stir with a fork until dry ingredients are moistened. Shape dough into a ball; cover and chill 1 hour.

Divide dough in half; store 1 portion in refrigerator. Roll remaining half of dough to ¼-inch thickness on a lightly floured surface. Cut with a 5-inch cowboy boot cookie cutter; carefully transfer to ungreased

Shapely Cheese Straws

◆ *You can substitute any size or shape of cutters for these spicy cheese straws called Cowboy Boots with a Kick (right). Adjust the baking time accordingly.*

baking sheets. Bake at 400° for 12 minute or until lightly browned. Let cool 1 minu on baking sheets. Carefully remove to wi racks to cool. Repeat with remainin dough. Yield: about 1 dozen.

Southwestern Salsa

2 cactus leaves (6 to 8 ounces)*
1 (15¼-ounce) can pineapple tidbits
    drained and coarsely chopped
1 (15-ounce) can black beans,
    rinsed and drained
¼ cup chopped fresh cilantro
¼ cup chopped purple onion
2 tablespoons finely chopped
    pickled jalapeño peppers
1 large clove garlic, minced
1 tablespoon sugar
2 tablespoons red wine vinegar
1 teaspoon grated lime rind
¾ teaspoon ground cumin
    Garnish: fresh cilantro sprig

Use a knife or vegetable peeler to remov prickles from cactus leaves; trim roug edges. Rinse and drain. Place cactus leave in a vegetable steamer over boiling wate Cover and steam 3 to 5 minutes or jus until crisp-tender. Let cool slightly, an coarsely chop.

Combine chopped cactus leaves, pine apple, beans, cilantro, onion, jalapeño pep per, and garlic; stir well. Combine suga vinegar, lime rind, and cumin. Add to cac tus mixture, tossing gently. Cover and chi thoroughly. Garnish, if desired. Serve wit assorted tortilla chips. Yield: 3 cups.

*Substitute ½ cup chopped green peppe for cactus leaves, if desired.

Sizzling Barbecue Sandwiches

1 medium onion, finely chopped
1 tablespoon olive oil
2 cups catsup
1 cup red wine vinegar
½ cup firmly packed dark brown
    sugar
¼ cup liquid smoke
¼ cup Worcestershire sauce
3 cloves garlic, minced
2 jalapeño peppers, minced
2 teaspoons salt
1 teaspoon coriander seeds,
    crushed
1 teaspoon cumin seeds, crushed
1 (4-pound) beef brisket
8 jumbo hamburger buns

Cook onion in hot oil in a medium saucepan, stirring constantly, until tender. Stir in catsup and next 4 ingredients. Combine garlic, jalapeño pepper, salt, coriander seeds, and cumin seeds; stir well. Add to sauce mixture. Simmer, uncovered, over medium-low heat for 15 minutes.

Trim excess fat from brisket. Place brisket on a sheet of heavy-duty aluminum foil in a roasting pan.

Spoon 1 cup sauce over brisket; seal foil around brisket. Bake at 325° for 3 to 3½ hours or until meat is very tender. Let cool slightly, and shred meat. Add 2 cups sauce to shredded meat. Serve on jumbo buns with remaining sauce. Yield: 8 servings.

Yellow Rose Pound Cake

    1 cup butter-flavored
      shortening
2½ cups sugar
    6 large eggs, separated
    ½ teaspoon baking soda
    1 cup buttermilk
2¾ cups all-purpose flour
    ½ teaspoon salt
    3 tablespoons bourbon
    ⅓ cup sugar
      Bourbon Sauce

Beat shortening at medium speed of an electric mixer about 2 minutes or until soft and creamy. Gradually add 2½ cups sugar, beating at medium speed 5 to 7 minutes. Add egg yolks, one at a time, beating just until yellow disappears.

Dissolve soda in buttermilk. Combine flour and salt; add to shortening mixture alternately with buttermilk mixture, beginning and ending with flour mixture. Mix at low speed just until blended after each addition. Stir in 3 tablespoons bourbon.

Beat egg whites at high speed of electric mixer until foamy; gradually add ⅓ cup sugar, 1 tablespoon at a time, beating until stiff peaks form and sugar dissolves (2 to 4 minutes). Gently fold egg whites into batter.

Pour batter into a greased and floured 10-inch tube pan. Bake at 350° for 1 hour and 15 minutes or until a wooden pick inserted in center comes out clean. Cool in pan on a wire rack 10 to 15 minutes; remove from pan, and place on a serving plate.

While cake is still warm, prick surface with a wooden pick at 1-inch intervals. Gradually pour Bourbon Sauce over cake. Yield: one 10-inch cake.

Bourbon Sauce
    ¾ cup sugar
    ½ cup butter or
      margarine
    ⅓ cup bourbon
    ¾ teaspoon vanilla extract

Yellow Rose Pound Cake

Combine sugar and butter in a small saucepan. Bring to a boil over medium heat. Boil mixture, stirring constantly, 3 minutes. Remove from heat, and let cool slightly. Stir in bourbon and vanilla. Yield: 1¼ cups.

Party Options

Before a football game, set up this tailgate feast in the stadium lot or a nearby field. The spicy menu will score points even before the gridiron action begins. Send fans off to the game with small brown bags of trailmix tied with rope—guaranteed to satisfy halftime munchies.

Autumn Lace Birthday Luncheon

Serves 6

Fruited Pork Salad

Sweet Potatoes with Bacon in Tangy Vinaigrette

Sautéed Sugar Snaps

Birthday Cake Laced with Love

Peach-Flavored Tea   Coffee

Combine autumn's glory with the delicacy of lace for this charming birthday celebration. Create a sentimental table by asking guests to bring a dinner plate of their favorite china; then during lunch, encourage everyone to share the special history of their china patterns. Lavish the table with dried hydrangeas and an antique lace tablecloth, and display antique jewelry, china, lace handkerchiefs, perfume bottles, and other vintage feminine keepsakes as the centerpiece. Decorate the honored guest's place setting with balloons, birthday cards, and lacy ribbon.

Birthday Cake Laced with Love (page 97)

Fruited Pork Salad

Lacy Trimmings

✦ *Set the mood for this birthday celebration with a handmade lace invitation and envelope (above and right). Write the invitations and addresses first; then glue lace over each invitation and envelope, using clear adhesive spray. Trim edges of lace.*

✦ *Suggest that each guest bring a gift of lace for the birthday girl.*

1½ pounds lean boneless pork loin
⅓ cup soy sauce
2 tablespoons peeled, grated gingerroot
2 cloves garlic, crushed
1 teaspoon ground cloves
3 cups cooked long-grain rice
1 cup chopped purple plums
½ cup green grapes, halved
3 green onions, diagonally sliced
2 small ripe starfruit, sliced (optional)
¼ cup lime juice
¼ cup soy sauce
2 tablespoons olive oil
2 tablespoons honey
2 heads Bibb lettuce

Slice pork into ¼-inch-thick slices. Arrange in a large shallow dish. Combine ⅓ cup soy sauce and next 3 ingredients; pour mixture over pork. Cover and marinate in refrigerator 30 minutes.

Drain pork, discarding marinade. Grill pork, covered, over medium-hot coals (350° to 400°) 2 to 3 minutes on each side or until done. Let pork cool, and slice into ¼-inch-wide strips.

Combine pork, rice, plums, grapes, green onions, and starfruit, if desired, in a large bowl; toss gently. Combine lime juice and next 3 ingredients; pour over salad. Cover and chill thoroughly. Serve salad in Bibb lettuce cups. Yield: 6 servings.

Sweet Potatoes with Bacon in Tangy Vinaigrette

3 medium-size sweet potatoes
   (about 2 pounds)
   Tangy Vinaigrette
6 slices bacon, cooked and
   coarsely crumbled
1 tablespoon chopped fresh parsley

Cook sweet potatoes in boiling water to
ver 30 to 35 minutes or just until tender.
rain and cool completely.
Peel potatoes; coarsely chop, and place in
erving bowl.
Pour Tangy Vinaigrette over sweet
tatoes, and toss gently. Sprinkle with

crumbled bacon and chopped parsley before
serving. Yield: 6 servings.

Tangy Vinaigrette
½ cup vegetable oil
¼ cup cider vinegar
3 tablespoons honey
½ teaspoon dry mustard
¼ teaspoon ground cumin
¼ teaspoon pepper

Combine all ingredients in a small jar;
cover tightly, and shake vigorously. Serve at
room temperature. Yield: about 1 cup.

Flowery Favors

✦ *Place a*
potpourri-covered
wreath under
each plate.
✦ *Attach a small*
clipping of dried
or silk flowers to
napkins at
each place setting
with lace ribbon.
✦ *Offer the*
wreaths and
flowers as
party favors.
✦ *Pork salad,*
sweet potatoes,
and sugar snaps
are the birthday
fare.

Gifts Galore

◆ *Lace napkins, place mats, lace-trimmed towels, lacy collars, pillows, lingerie, stationery, barrettes, socks, gloves, and jewelry offer theme-related ideas for birthday gifts.*

Sautéed Sugar Snaps

3 cups fresh Sugar Snap peas (1 pound) or 2 (10-ounce) package frozen Sugar Snap peas, thawed
1 tablespoon olive oil
¼ teaspoon salt
¼ teaspoon freshly ground pepper

Wash pea pods, and trim stem ends.
Cook pea pods in hot oil in a large skill over medium-high heat, stirring constantl 30 seconds to 1 minute or just until cris tender. Sprinkle with salt and pepper. Yiel 6 servings.

Birthday Cake Laced with Love

Birthday Cake Laced with Love

¾ cup butter, softened
½ (8-ounce) package cream cheese, softened
½ cups sugar
3 large eggs
¾ cup sour cream
1 teaspoon baking soda
¾ cups sifted cake flour
2 teaspoons vanilla or almond extract
 Velvet Glaze
½ cup cream cheese-flavored ready-to-spread frosting

Beat butter and cream cheese at medium speed of an electric mixer 5 minutes or until creamy; gradually add sugar, beating well. Add eggs, one at a time, beating after each addition.

Combine sour cream and soda; let stand minutes. Add flour to creamed mixture alternately with sour cream mixture, beginning and ending with flour. Mix after each addition. Stir in flavoring.

Pour batter into a greased and floured -inch springform pan or 9-inch round cakepan with 3-inch sides. Bake at 325° for 5 minutes to 1 hour or until a wooden pick inserted in center comes out clean. Cool in pan on a wire rack 10 minutes; remove from pan, and let cool completely on wire rack. Place wax paper under wire rack. Pour Velvet Glaze over cake, letting excess drip down sides of cake onto wax paper. Let cake stand until glaze is set.

Spoon cream cheese frosting into a zip-top plastic bag; remove air and seal bag. Snip a tiny hole in 1 corner of bag, and pipe frosting over cake in a decorative lacy design. Yield: one 9-inch cake.

Velvet Glaze

⅔ cup whipping cream
2 tablespoons light corn syrup
6 ounces bittersweet chocolate, finely chopped
1 teaspoon vanilla extract

Combine whipping cream and corn syrup in a medium saucepan; bring to a simmer over medium heat. Remove from heat, and add chocolate. Let stand 1 minute. Stir gently until chocolate melts completely. Stir in vanilla. Let glaze cool. Yield: enough glaze for one 9-inch cake.

Party Options

You can adapt this birthday theme to an Autumn Lace Wedding Shower for a bride-to-be. Gifts of lace (especially lingerie) are perfect for an intended bride.

Fall Tablescapes

Decorate your table with these one-of-a-kind collections that celebrate the colorful fruits and flowers of the season.

Pause for Pottery

Build a sideboard decoration around treasured pieces of pottery. Gather together an eclectic mix of old and new pottery. Coffee mugs and pitchers make creative vases for branches of persimmons, crabapples, berries, or dried flowers. Fill bowls with polished apples, and display pears on a pedestal. A favorite platter provides a fitting background.

The Copper Corner

Mix copper cookware and brass accessories in this rich tablescape. Fill a chafing dish or colander with multicolored peppers. Add measuring cups and spoons, cookie cutters, a grater, stockpot, candy mold, and an assortment of pitchers. Bittersweet berries offer a colorful reminder of the season's beauty.

Harvest Bounty

Stack baskets and wooden produce crates, and load them with autumn's harvest. Include pomegranates, miniature pumpkins, gourds, and a spray of very autumn leaves.

Tins for the Table

Show off a collection of antique tins by turning them into table decorations. Fill tins of different sizes and shapes with seasonal candies and fresh or dried flowers.

Romantic Anniversary Dinner

Serves 2

Tossed Green Salad

Tenderloin for Two
With Peppercorn Cream

Hot Cooked Rice

Green Beans with Crispy Shallots

Red Wine

Fudge Pie
With Peanut Butter Sauce

Champagne   Coffee

Proclaim your love for that special
someone with this romantic feast.
To create ambience, stack large fluffy
pillows near a roaring fire, and add soft
background music and the warm glow of
scented candles. Dazzle the one you love
with a message scripted on a plate in chocolate.
Tie champagne flutes together with ribbon,
and end the meal with a special toast.

Fudge Pie with Peanut Butter Sauce (page 103)

Tenderloin for Two
With Peppercorn Cream

1 tablespoon olive oil
2 (6-ounce) beef tenderloin steaks
  Salt
  Pepper
¼ cup brandy
1 large clove garlic, minced
1 teaspoon multicolored
    peppercorns, crushed
½ teaspoon dried oregano
⅛ teaspoon salt
⅔ cup whipping cream
1½ tablespoons sour cream
  Hot cooked rice
  Garnish: fresh oregano sprigs

Heat olive oil in a medium skillet until hot. Sprinkle tenderloin steaks with salt and pepper. Sear tenderloin steaks on both sid[es] in skillet. Remove from skillet, and place [on] a rack in a broiler pan. Broil 5½ inch[es] from heat (with electric oven door partial[ly] opened) 5 to 7 minutes on each side [or] until meat thermometer registers 140[°] (rare), 150° (medium-rare), or 160° (medium[).

Add brandy to drippings in skillet; brin[g] to a boil, and deglaze pan by scraping part[i]cles that cling to bottom. Add minced ga[r]lic, peppercorns, oregano, and salt; cook [1] minute. Add whipping cream; bring to [a] boil, and cook 6 to 7 minutes or until sauc[e] is reduced by half. Remove from hea[t.] Whisk in sour cream, and spoon sauce ov[er] steaks. Serve with rice. Garnish, if desire[d.] Yield: 2 servings.

Green Beans with Crispy Shallots

1 shallot
1 (10-ounce) package frozen
    French-cut green beans, thawed
3 tablespoons boiling water
1 tablespoon butter or margarine
1 tablespoon sliced pimiento
2 teaspoons balsamic vinegar
¼ teaspoon salt
¼ teaspoon sugar
¼ teaspoon pepper
1 tablespoon butter or margarine

Slice shallot lengthwise into very thi[n] slivers; set aside. Place beans in a skille[t] dd boiling water; cover and cook 2 minutes over medium heat. Uncover and stir in tablespoon butter, pimiento, vinegar, salt, ugar, and pepper. Sauté 1 minute.

Transfer bean mixture to a small serving late. Add remaining 1 tablespoon butter to skillet. Add slivered shallot, and cook over medium-high heat until crisp and browned. Remove with a slotted spoon, and drain on paper towels. Sprinkle browned shallot over beans, and serve immediately. Yield: 2 servings.

Fudge Pie with Peanut Butter Sauce

¼ cups chocolate wafer crumbs
⅓ cup butter or margarine, melted
½ cup butter or margarine, softened
½ cup firmly packed brown sugar
3 large eggs
1 (12-ounce) package semisweet chocolate morsels, melted
1 teaspoon vanilla extract
½ cup all-purpose flour
¾ cup chopped, unsalted peanuts
2 (1-ounce) squares semisweet chocolate, melted and cooled
Peanut Butter Sauce
Frozen whipped topping, thawed
Toasted, chopped peanuts

Combine chocolate wafer crumbs and ⅓ up melted butter; press mixture firmly on ottom and up sides of a 9-inch pieplate. Bake at 350° for 6 to 8 minutes.

Beat ½ cup butter at medium speed of n electric mixer until creamy. Gradually dd sugar, beating mixture until blended. Add eggs, one at a time, beating after each ddition. Stir in melted chocolate morsels nd vanilla. Add flour, beating at low speed ust until blended. Stir in ¾ cup peanuts.

Pour chocolate mixture into prepared rust. Bake at 350° for 28 minutes; let cool n a wire rack.

Spoon remaining 2 ounces melted chocolate into a small zip-top plastic bag or a small squeeze bottle with a narrow tip. If using a plastic bag, snip a tiny hole in bottom corner, using scissors. Write "Happy Anniversary" in chocolate around the rim of a large plate.

To serve, slice pie, and place 1 slice on prepared plate. Top with Peanut Butter Sauce, whipped topping, and additional chopped peanuts. Yield: one 9-inch pie.

Peanut Butter Sauce

¼ cup firmly packed brown sugar
3 tablespoons butter or margarine
2 tablespoons light corn syrup
½ cup crunchy peanut butter
⅓ cup whipping cream
1 large egg, slightly beaten
2 teaspoons vanilla extract

Combine brown sugar, butter, and corn syrup in a small heavy saucepan. Bring to a boil, stirring frequently.

Stir in peanut butter and whipping cream, and cook 2 minutes. Gradually add one-fourth of hot mixture to egg, stirring constantly. Add to remaining hot mixture. Cook, stirring constantly, 1 minute or until mixture reaches 160°. Remove from heat, and add vanilla. Let cool. Yield 1⅓ cups.

Romantic Writing

✦ Present this luscious dessert with words of love handwritten across the plate. To allow plenty of room for your message, choose an oversized dinner plate or charger.

Halloween Barn Party

Serves 10

Curly Pigtails

Brewing Stew in a Pumpkin

Spiderweb Apples

Corny Candy on a Stick

Hot Apple Cider

Ghosts and goblins will envy this Halloween party which takes place down on the farm. Children, dressed in farm animal costumes, can nibble on Curly Pigtails, while adults enjoy the warming blend of flavors in the hearty stew. Use apple baskets lined with bandanas as trick or treat containers; fill them with sweet treats like Spiderweb Apples and Corny Candy on a Stick. Gather the children in the barn after dark for ghost stories, farm tales, and bobbing for apples. A hayride completes the evening.

A painted wagon, bales of hay, pumpkins, crates, and baskets set the scene for children of all ages to experience trick or treating with a new twist.

Curly Pigtails

10 (12-inch) wooden skewers
10 all-beef frankfurters
½ cup prepared mustard
2 teaspoons brown sugar
1 teaspoon curry powder
1 (8-ounce) can refrigerated
    crescent dinner rolls

Curly Pigtails

Insert a wooden skewer into 1 end of each frankfurter, leaving 7 inches of each skewer exposed. Combine mustard, sugar, and curry powder, stirring well.

Unroll crescent roll dough, and shape into a 12- x 8-inch rectangle. Press perforations to seal. Cut rectangle evenly into 10 (8-inch-long) strips.

Brush 1 side of each strip with mustard mixture. Wrap 1 strip around each frankfurter, mustard side in, leaving ¾-inch of the frankfurter exposed as dough forms spiral. Place on an ungreased baking sheet. Bake at 375° for 10 to 12 minutes or until golden. Serve with remaining mustard mixture. Yield: 10 servings.

Bewitching Brew

✦ *To use a small pumpkin as a tureen (above), remove the top of the pumpkin, and hollow out the insides. Spoon in the stew, replace the top, and keep in a warm oven until ready to serve.*
✦ *Or, serve this piping hot stew from a black cast-iron kettle that resembles a boiling caldron.*

Brewing Stew in a Pumpkin

½ cup all-purpose flour
2 teaspoons cracked pepper
2½ pounds beef for stewing, cubed
¼ cup olive oil
3 small onions, quartered
3 cloves garlic, minced
3 bay leaves
1 `tablespoon dried thyme
4 cups water
2 (10½-ounce) cans condensed beef
    broth, undiluted
4 large carrots, scraped and sliced
3 large potatoes, peeled and cut
    into chunks
1 (10-ounce) package frozen English
    peas

Combine flour and cracked pepper. Dredge beef cubes in flour mixture.

Heat oil in a large Dutch oven until hot; add beef, and cook until browned on all sides. Add any remaining flour from dredging, onions, garlic, bay leaves, thyme, water, and beef broth.

Bring mixture to a boil; cover, reduce heat, and simmer 2 hours.

Add carrots, potatoes, and peas. Bring to a boil; reduce heat, and simmer, uncovered, 30 minutes or until vegetables are tender and stew is thickened.

Remove and discard bay leaves. Serve stew in a hollowed-out pumpkin, if desired. Yield: 4 quarts.

Spiderweb Apples

10   medium apples
10   wooden craft sticks
 2   (14-ounce) bags caramels
⅓   cup water
½   cups coarsely crushed, salted thin
        pretzel sticks
 1   (16-ounce) container
        ready-to-spread chocolate
        frosting
 1   (16-ounce) container
        ready-to-spread vanilla
        frosting

Wash and dry apples. Remove stems, and insert wooden craft sticks into stem ends of apples. Set aside.

Combine caramels and water in a large saucepan. Cook over medium-low heat until smooth, stirring frequently. Remove from heat.

Dip apples into hot caramel, spooning caramel mixture over apples to coat completely. Scrape excess caramel from bottom of each apple; roll coated apples in crushed pretzels. Place apples on greased wax paper on a tray. Refrigerate at least 15 minutes or until caramel is set.

Spoon chocolate frosting into a small heavy-duty, zip-top plastic bag; seal bag. Submerge bag in a small saucepan of hot water until frosting is thin enough to pipe. Remove bag from saucepan.

Snip a tiny hole in 1 corner of bag, using scissors. Drizzle warm chocolate in a webbed design over each apple. Repeat heating and drizzling procedure with vanilla frosting.

Chill apples until firm. Wrap apples in cellophane wrap. Tie with heavy string. Yield: 10 servings.

Spiderweb Apples

Popcorn Pops

✦ *For trick or treaters, wrap Corny Candy on a Stick in cellophane and tie with raffia.*

Corny Candy on a Stick

50 large marshmallows
⅓ cup butter or margarine, cut up
20 cups popped corn
2 cups teddy bear-shaped chocolate graham cracker cookies
2½ cups candy corn
Vegetable cooking spray
20 wooden craft sticks

Combine marshmallows and butter in a large Dutch oven. Cook over medium-low heat until marshmallows melt, stirring occasionally. Remove mixture from heat.

Combine popped corn and graham cracker cookies in a large bowl. Pour marshmallow mixture over popped corn mixture, tossing to coat. Add candy corn; stir well.

Coat hands with cooking spray. Shape popped corn mixture into 3-inch balls. Insert a wooden craft stick into each popcorn ball. Let cool on wax paper. Wrap balls in cellophane. Yield: 20 popcorn balls.

Party Options

If you aren't near a farm or barn, create this barn party setting in a church or school gym, a garage, or a large basement. Just bring in bales of hay, leaves and grass, and some safe barnyard tools to create the scene.

"No Sweat" Costumes

Make these Halloween costumes from children's sweat suits. They're
so quick and easy—just be sure to allow time for the glue to dry.

Bessie the Cow

Glue black felt cutouts onto a white sweat suit,
using an electric glue gun. Wear black mittens
and turn black socks down over shoes for
hooves. Glue matching ears onto a headband.
Purchase a rubber nose from a variety store.

Prissy the Pig

Attach two small pillow forms to inside front
and back of a pink sweatshirt. Cut pointed ears
from pink felt; stiffen ears with spray
starch, and glue onto a pink headband.
Make a curly tail from pink pipe clean-
ers, and pin from inside sweatpants.
Purchase a rubber snout from a
variety store.

Quacky Duck

Purchase feathers from a variety store. Attach
feathers to a yellow sweat suit, using an electric
glue gun. Glue feathers onto an orange baseball
cap for the bill. Cut webbed feet from orange
felt; attach with elastic over shoes.

Fred the Barnyard Dog

Choose a brown, black, or gray sweat suit. Glue
felt cutouts onto sweat suit, using an electric
glue gun. Cut floppy ears from two large pieces
of felt; attach the ears to a piece of elastic. Use
face paint to add whiskers and a nose.

Camouflaged Covered-Dish Dinner

Serves 10

Baked Stuffed Quail With Tomato Jam

Duck and Sausage Gumbo

Venison Chili

Commercial French Bread

Red Wine   Beer   Iced Tea

Commercial Cheesecake

Coffee

Herald the thrill of the hunt with this potluck supper featuring a variety of wild game entrées. A rustic setting and casual camouflage attire suit the occasion. Bring the great outdoors inside with a centerpiece of pinecones, tree stumps, birdhouses, autumn leaves and berries, and incorporate deer horns, lanterns, and rough-hewn baskets. Serve drinks in mason jars and the entrées in pewter bowls and plates. Use slingshots and tiny birdhouse ornaments as unique napkin rings.

From left: Hot cooked rice, Venison Chili (page 115), Duck and Sausage Gumbo (page 114), French bread

Baked Stuffed Quail with Tomato Jam

Camouflage Quips

◆ *Hand-carved slingshots, bird-house ornaments, and miniature lanterns make whimsical favors (below).*

◆ *Tie twig flatware and pewter spoons together with twine.*

◆ *Collect old pie tins from a tag sale or antique shop to serve as inexpensive, rustic dinner plates.*

½ pound ground pork sausage
1 teaspoon ground ginger
  Bacon-Pecan Cornbread Loaf
½ cup toasted, finely chopped pecans
½ cup chopped dried apricots
¾ cup Riesling wine, divided
10 quail, dressed
½ cup all-purpose flour
½ teaspoon salt
½ teaspoon pepper
¼ cup plus 2 tablespoons butter or margarine
  Garnish: fresh parsley sprigs
  Tomato Jam

Combine sausage and ginger. Brown sausage mixture in a large skillet, stirring until it crumbles. Remove from heat, and set aside.

Slice ends from Bacon-Pecan Cornbread Loaf, and crumble enough to measure 1 cup. Slice remaining cornbread into 10 slices, and set aside.

Combine sausage mixture, cornbread crumbs, pecans, and apricots; stir well. Sprinkle with ¼ cup wine, stirring well.

Rinse quail thoroughly with cold water, pat dry. Spoon ¼ cup stuffing mixture into body cavity of each quail. Secure each cavity with wooden picks, and tie legs together with string.

Combine flour, salt, and pepper; dredge stuffed quail in flour mixture. Melt butter in a large heavy skillet. Add quail, and brown on both sides.

Remove quail from skillet, and arrange in a 13- x 9- x 2-inch pan. Add remaining ½ cup wine to drippings in skillet; bring to a boil, and deglaze skillet by scraping particles that cling to bottom. Remove from heat, and spoon over quail. Cover and bake at 350° for 45 minutes.

Toast cornbread slices, and cut into triangles. Arrange cornbread around quail on a platter; garnish, if desired. Serve with Tomato Jam. Yield: 10 servings.

Bacon-Pecan Cornbread Loaf

4 slices bacon
  Vegetable oil
¾ cup chopped pecans
1½ cups yellow cornmeal
1¼ cups all-purpose flour
⅓ cup sugar
1½ teaspoons baking soda
½ teaspoon salt
2 large eggs, lightly beaten
1 cup buttermilk
  Yellow cornmeal

Cook bacon in a large skillet until crisp; crumble bacon, and set aside. Pour bacon

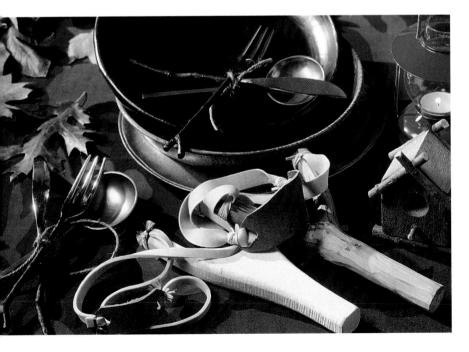

Quail
Caucus

✦ *Toasted corn-*
bread triangles
embellish the
platter of
glazed quail (left).
✦ *Encourage*
guests to wear
camouflage attire
to the party.
✦ *Ask guests to*
share copies of
their recipes for
wild game.

rippings into a measuring cup; add enough vegetable oil to drippings to measure ½ cup, and set aside. Add pecans to skillet; cook over medium heat until browned, stirring frequently. Set pecans aside.

Combine 1½ cups cornmeal and next 4 ingredients in a large bowl. Combine eggs and buttermilk; stir in reserved drippings. Add to cornmeal mixture, and stir just until dry ingredients are moistened. Fold in reserved bacon and pecans.

Grease a 9- x 5- x 3-inch loafpan; dust with cornmeal. Pour batter into prepared pan. Bake at 325° for 50 minutes or until a wooden pick inserted in center comes out clean. Cool in pan on a wire rack 30 minutes; remove from pan, and let cool completely. Yield: one 9-inch loaf.

Tomato Jam

¼ cup olive oil
1½ cups finely chopped onion
1 pound Roma tomatoes, diced
⅔ cup finely chopped dried apricots
¼ cup apricot nectar
1 tablespoon brown sugar
2 to 4 tablespoons dry sherry
½ teaspoon salt
½ teaspoon ground ginger
½ teaspoon pepper

Heat oil in a saucepan over medium-high heat. Add onion, and cook until tender. Add tomato and remaining ingredients; stir well. Reduce heat, and simmer, uncovered, 15 minutes or until thickened. Serve warm or at room temperature. Yield: 3 cups.

Duck and Sausage Gumbo

1 (5- to 6-pound) duck, dressed
   and skinned
2 stalks celery with leaves, cut into
   pieces
1 large carrot, cut into pieces
1 large onion, quartered
1½ cups all-purpose flour
1 teaspoon ground red pepper
1 teaspoon paprika
¾ teaspoon dry mustard
¾ teaspoon ground white pepper
¾ teaspoon black pepper
½ teaspoon salt
1 cup vegetable oil
2 cups chopped green pepper
2 cups chopped onion
2 cups chopped celery
2 tablespoons minced garlic
4 cups chopped smoked sausage
   (about 1¼ pounds)
1 (16-ounce) package frozen sliced
   okra
1 bay leaf
   Hot cooked rice

Place duck in a Dutch oven; add water t[o] cover. Bring water to a boil. Skim off foam Add celery pieces, carrot, and quartere[d] onion. Cover, reduce heat, and simmer [1] hour. Remove duck from broth, reserving [8] cups broth. Discard vegetables. Set mea[t] and broth aside to cool. Remove meat fro[m] bones, and chop into bite-size pieces.

Combine flour and next 6 ingredients stir well. Heat oil in Dutch oven or larg[e] cast-iron skillet. Add flour mixture, an[d] cook over medium heat, stirring constantl[y] until roux is chocolate colored (about 30 t[o] 45 minutes). Reduce heat to medium-lo[w] add green pepper, chopped onion, choppe[d] celery, and garlic. Cook, stirring constantl[y] until vegetables are tender.

Gradually add reserved broth to rou[x] stirring well. Add chopped duck mea[t] sausage, okra, and bay leaf. Bring to a boi[l] reduce heat, and simmer, uncovered, 5[0] minutes. Remove and discard bay lea[f] Serve gumbo with hot cooked rice an[d] French bread. Yield: 3½ quarts.

Gumbo with Gusto

◆ *French bread and cold beer make the spicy Duck and Sausage Gumbo course complete.*

Venison Chili

½ pound mild Italian sausage
8 slices bacon
1½ pounds coarsely ground venison
2 large onions, chopped
2 large green peppers, seeded and
   chopped
3 cloves garlic, minced
2 jalapeño peppers, seeded and
   chopped
2 dried chili peppers, crumbled
1½ tablespoons chili powder
1 teaspoon ground cumin
1 teaspoon dried oregano
½ teaspoon salt
1 (14½-ounce) can whole tomatoes,
   undrained and chopped
1 (12-ounce) can tomato paste
1 (12-ounce) can beer
1 (16-ounce) can pinto beans, drained
   Garnishes: sour cream, sliced
   green onions, shredded Monterey
   Jack cheese, sliced ripe olives

Brown sausage in a large Dutch oven over medium heat. Drain on paper towels, and slice.

Cook bacon in Dutch oven until crisp; remove bacon, reserving half the drippings. Crumble bacon, and set aside.

Heat reserved drippings over medium heat until hot. Add venison, onions, green peppers, and garlic. Cook until meat is browned and vegetables are tender, stirring often. Add reserved sausage, bacon, jalapeño peppers, and next 8 ingredients; stir well. Bring to a boil; cover, reduce heat, and simmer 45 minutes, stirring often. Add beans during the last 15 minutes of cooking. Garnish, if desired. Yield: 11 cups.

Venison Chili

Party Options

Adapt this Camouflaged Covered-Dish Dinner to a rip-roaring birthday bash for an avid hunter or outdoorsman. Include a note on the invitation for each guest to bring a "wild and woolly" gag gift for the birthday boy.

A Blessed Thanksgiving

Serves 8

Roast Turkey with Pear and
Hazelnut Stuffing

Cranberry Sauce

Mashed Potatoes   Steamed Broccoli

Marmalade Candied Carrots

Commercial Dinner Rolls

Water   Wine

White Chocolate Tart
With Pecan Crust

Sweet Potato Pie
With Gingersnap Streusel

Coffee

Giving thanks comes naturally
when generations of family
gather for this blessed feast. Create a centerpiece
for your table using tapestries, braided rope,
marbled pedestals overflowing with gilded fruits
and vegetables, and an open hymnal presenting a
hymn like "Blessed Be The Tie That Binds."

Among the table's fineries are handmade
place cards and cherub candlestick holders.

Roast Turkey with Pear and Hazelnut Stuffing

1 (12-pound) turkey
Fresh sage leaves (optional)
Pear and Hazelnut Stuffing
⅓ cup butter or margarine, melted
⅓ cup all-purpose flour
1½ cups turkey or chicken broth, divided
1 teaspoon freshly ground pepper
¾ teaspoon poultry seasoning
½ teaspoon salt
Garnish: fresh sage leaves

Remove giblets and neck, and rinse turkey thoroughly with cold water; pat dry. Tuck several fresh sage leaves under skin of bird, if desired. Lightly pack 1½ cups Pear and Hazelnut Stuffing into neck cavity of turkey. Lightly pack 5 cups stuffing into body cavity. Tuck legs under flap of skin around tail, or close cavity with skewers, and truss. Tie ends of legs to tail with cord. Lift wingtips up and over back, and tuck under turkey.

Place turkey in a lightly greased roasting pan, breast side up; brush entire bird with melted butter. Insert meat thermometer into meaty portion of thigh, making sure it does not touch bone. Bake at 325° for 3 to 3½ hours or until meat thermometer registers 180°. Baste turkey frequently with remaining melted butter and pan juices. If turkey starts to brown too much, cover with aluminum foil.

When turkey is two-thirds done, cut the cord or band of skin holding the drumstick ends to the tail; this will ensure that the insides of the thighs are cooked. Turkey is done when drumsticks are easy to move up and down. Transfer turkey to a serving platter. Let turkey stand 15 minutes before carving.

Combine flour and ½ cup broth; stir until smooth. Add to drippings in roasting pan. Bring to a boil over medium heat, stirring constantly. (Place pan over 2 burners if necessary.) Stir in remaining broth, pepper, poultry seasoning, and salt. Reduce heat, and simmer 5 minutes or until gravy is thickened, stirring frequently.

Serve turkey with Pear and Hazelnut Stuffing and gravy. Garnish, if desired. Yield: 12 servings.

Pear and Hazelnut Stuffing

1 pound ground pork sausage
4 stalks celery, sliced
1 large onion, chopped
½ cup butter or margarine, melted
2 large red pears, chopped
4 cloves garlic, minced
1 (16-ounce) loaf day-old French
   bread, cubed
1 cup toasted, chopped hazelnuts
3 tablespoons chopped fresh sage or
   1 tablespoon rubbed sage
2 teaspoons coarsely ground pepper
½ cups turkey or chicken broth

Brown pork sausage in a large skillet, stirring until it crumbles. Drain sausage on paper towels. Discard drippings. Sauté celery and onion in butter in large skillet over medium-high heat just until crisp-tender. Add chopped pear and garlic; sauté until pear is tender. Remove sautéed mixture from heat.

Place French bread cubes in a large bowl. Stir in sausage, celery mixture, hazelnuts, sage, and pepper. Pour broth over stuffing, stirring gently. Stuff turkey, using 6½ cups stuffing.

Place remaining stuffing in a lightly greased 8-inch square pan. Bake, uncovered, at 325° during the last hour the turkey bakes. Yield: 11 cups.

Note: If you purchase a frozen turkey, allow three days for it to thaw in refrigerator.

Blessings and Beyond

◆ Roast Turkey with Pear and Hazelnut Stuffing and Marmalade Candied Carrots are highlights on the plate.

◆ Copy a Thanksgiving sketch onto parchment paper for place cards.

◆ Pass a "blessings book" of blank pages (far left) around the table for each family member to record special memories. Later add poignant photographs of the day, and keep the book in a special place so relatives can enjoy it in years ahead.

Marmalade Candied Carrots

Elegance in Print

◆ *Present the Thanksgiving menu in calligraphy in a decorative frame on the table or in the foyer.*

2 pounds carrots, scraped and slice⋯ diagonally
⅔ cup orange marmalade
2 tablespoons brown sugar
2 tablespoons butter or margarine
3 tablespoons spiced rum
½ cup coarsely chopped pecans, toasted

Arrange carrots in a vegetable steame⋯ over boiling water. Cover and steam 1⋯ minutes or until crisp-tender.

Transfer carrots to a serving bowl. Gentl⋯ stir marmalade into carrots until mar⋯ malade melts.

Combine brown sugar, butter, and ru⋯ in a small saucepan. Cook over mediu⋯ heat until butter and brown sugar mel⋯ Remove from heat, and stir in pecans. Pou⋯ over carrot mixture in bowl. Toss gentl⋯ Serve with a slotted spoon. Yield: 8 servings.

White Chocolate Tart with Pecan Crust

18 pecan shortbread cookies, crushed
¾ cup finely chopped pecans
¼ cup butter or margarine, melted
2 (1-ounce) squares semisweet chocolate
1 tablespoon shortening
16 pecan halves
½ cup whipping cream
9 ounces premium white chocolate, finely chopped
1½ cups (12 ounces) mascarpone cheese
3 tablespoons Frangelico liqueur
1¼ cups whipping cream

Combine cookie crumbs, chopped pecans, and melted butter; stir well. Press mixture in bottom and up sides of a⋯ 11-inch tart pan with removable bottom⋯ Bake at 375° for 8 minutes. Let cool.

Combine semisweet chocolate and short⋯ ening in top of a double boiler; bring wate⋯ to a boil. Reduce heat to low; cook unt⋯ chocolate melts. Dip 8 pecan halves halfwa⋯ into chocolate mixture. Let harden on⋯ wire rack. Brush remaining chocolate mix⋯ ture over prepared crust. Let cool completel⋯

Place ½ cup whipping cream in top of⋯ double boiler over hot, not simmering⋯ water. Heat whipping cream thoroughl⋯ Gradually add white chocolate, and stir con⋯ stantly with a spatula until white chocolat⋯

White Chocolate Tart with Pecan Crust

melts. Remove from heat. Let cool to room temperature. Dip remaining 8 pecan halves halfway into white chocolate mixture. Let harden on wire rack. Dip again, if desired. Let remaining white chocolate mixture cool completely.

Position knife blade in food processor bowl; add mascarpone cheese and Frangelico. Process 10 seconds (mixture may look curdled). Add white chocolate mixture; process 30 seconds or until smooth. Slowly pour 1¼ cups whipping cream through food chute with processor running, blending 2 to 3 minutes or until mixture is very smooth, scraping down sides of processor bowl occasionally.

Spoon mixture into prepared crust. Cover and chill tart 8 hours. Top with chocolate-dipped pecan halves and white chocolate-dipped pecan halves. Let tart stand at room temperature 5 minutes before serving. Yield: one 11-inch tart.

Sweet Potato Pie with Gingersnap Streusel

2 cups gingersnap crumbs

1/3 cup butter or margarine, melted

1 (29-ounce) can sweet potatoes, drained and mashed

1 1/4 cups evaporated milk

3/4 cup firmly packed brown sugar

3 large eggs, beaten

1 1/4 teaspoons ground cinnamon

1 teaspoon ground allspice

2/3 cup coarsely crushed gingersnaps

1/3 cup firmly packed brown sugar

3 tablespoons all-purpose flour

2 tablespoons butter or margarine, cut up

Garnish: sweetened whipped cream

Combine 2 cups gingersnap crumbs an 1/3 cup melted butter; stir well. Firmly pres crumb mixture over bottom and up sides c a 9 1/2-inch deep-dish pieplate. Bake at 350 for 6 to 8 minutes. Let cool.

Combine sweet potatoes and next ingredients; stir well with a wire whisk. Pou sweet potato mixture into prepared crust Bake at 350° for 20 minutes.

Combine 2/3 cup crushed gingersnaps, 1/ cup brown sugar, and flour; cut in 2 table spoons butter with a pastry blender unt mixture is crumbly. Sprinkle streusel ove pie, and bake an additional 15 minutes Cover pie with aluminum foil, and bake a additional 25 minutes or until set. Let coc on a wire rack. Garnish, if desired. Yield one 9 1/2-inch deep-dish pie.

Gilded Glory

✦ *Sweet Potato Pie with Gingersnap Streusel looks particularly rich nestled among gilded fruit.*

✦ *To make gilded objects, dry fruit, berries, and pinecones with a cloth. Spray them with two coats of metallic gold or copper spray paint. (Gilded fruit is for decoration only.)*

Leftover Turkey at Its Best

Use your leftover turkey in this thick, rich stew.
Hollow out small bread loaves to make delicious edible bowls.

Turkey Stew in a Bread Bowl

6 (7½-inch) sourdough
    sub rolls or (8-ounce)
    round loaves
    sourdough bread
2 cups chopped carrot
2 tablespoons butter or
    margarine, melted
2 large baking potatoes,
    peeled and chopped
1 large onion, chopped
2 cups water
2 (10¾-ounce) cans cream
    of mushroom soup
1 (12-ounce) can
    evaporated milk
2 bay leaves
2 teaspoons dried thyme
3 cups chopped cooked
    leftover turkey
1 (10-ounce) package
    frozen English peas
1 cup (4 ounces) shredded
    mozzarella cheese

Using a serrated knife, hollow out the center of each loaf to form a ¾-inch-thick shell. Place hollow loaves on a baking sheet. Bake at 350° for 15 minutes.

Cook carrot in butter in a Dutch oven over medium-high heat, stirring constantly, 4 to 5 minutes. Add potatoes and next 6 ingredients.

Bring mixture to a boil; cover, reduce heat, and simmer 30 minutes or until vegetables are tender, stirring often. Stir in turkey, peas, and cheese.

Simmer, uncovered, an additional 5 minutes. Remove and discard bay leaves.

To serve, ladle stew into individual bread bowls. (Tear off pieces of the bread bowl to dip in stew as you eat.) Yield: 6 servings.

WIN

T E R

Nutcracker Sweet Swap

Serves 12

Nutty Brownies

Chocolate Crunch Cheesecake

Easy Roasted Nut Clusters

Frosted Fruitcake Bars

Stained Glass Divinity

Toasted Almond and
Cranberry Cookies

Benne Seed Brittle

Coffee Bar

*H*ost a dessert swap featuring
The Nutcracker as your theme.
This Christmas classic lends Tchaikovsky's
famous score as enchanting background music
for your party and provides ideas
for decorating, too. Display a variety of
nutcrackers on your table and a wreath made
from nuts on the wall or front door. Ask friends
to bring their favorite nutty dessert, along
with copies of the recipe.

Top left on pedestal: Chocolate Crunch Cheesecake; and on
platter, Frosted Fruitcake Bars, Toasted Almond and
Cranberry Cookies, Easy Roasted Nut Clusters, Stained
Glass Divinity (pages 129-131)

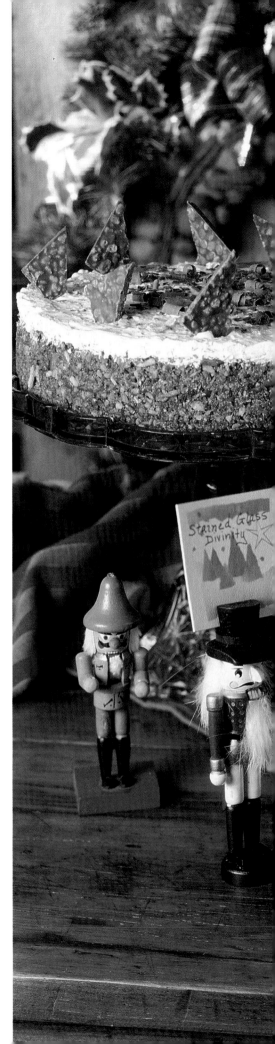

◆ *Nutty*
Brownies (right)
taste best when
accompanied by a
cup of freshly
perked java.
◆ *Serve a variety*
of nutty flavored
coffees in keeping
with the party
theme.
◆ *Offer flavored*
creamers and
syrups as part of
the coffee bar.
◆ *Identify*
flavored creamers
on tiny cards
inserted in
nutcracker place
card holders.

Nutty Brownies

  1 cup quick-cooking oats, uncooked
1¼ cups all-purpose flour, divided
  ½ cup firmly packed brown sugar
  ½ cup butter or margarine, melted
  ¼ teaspoon salt
  ⅓ cup butter or margarine
  2 (1-ounce) squares unsweetened
      chocolate
  2 large eggs
  1 cup sugar
  1 teaspoon vanilla extract
  ¾ cup chopped macadamia nuts
      Creamy Frosting
      Chocolate-Coated Macadamias

Combine oats, ½ cup flour, brown sugar, ½ cup melted butter, and salt. Stir until blended. Spread in a greased 9-inch square pan. Bake at 350° for 10 minutes.

Combine ⅓ cup butter and chocolate in a small saucepan; cook over medium-low heat until melted, stirring frequently.

Beat eggs at medium speed of an electric mixer until thick and pale. Add 1 cup sugar and vanilla; stir well. Stir in melted chocolate mixture, remaining ¾ cup flour, and ¾ cup macadamia nuts. Spread over crust.

Bake at 350° for 25 minutes. Let coo completely on a wire rack. Spread Cream Frosting over brownies. Cut into 1 squares. Top each with a Chocolate-Coate Macadamia. Yield: 16 brownies.

Creamy Frosting

  2 cups sifted powdered sugar
  ¼ cup butter or margarine,
      softened
1½ tablespoons milk

Combine powdered sugar, butter, an milk in a small bowl. Beat at high speed an electric mixer just until smooth. Yiel about 1 cup.

Chocolate-Coated Macadamias

  ¼ cup semisweet chocolate morsels
16 macadamia nuts

Melt morsels over low heat in a sma heavy saucepan, stirring frequently. Remo from heat; let cool slightly. Dip eac macadamia nut halfway into melted choco late. Place on wax paper to dry. Yiel 16 coated nuts.

Chocolate Crunch Cheesecake

½ cup butter or margarine

1 (1-ounce) square semisweet
    chocolate

½ cups crushed unsalted pretzels

½ cup finely chopped pecans

3 tablespoons sugar

1 (8-ounce) package cream cheese,
    softened

1 (3-ounce) package cream cheese,
    softened

⅔ cup sugar

5 large eggs

8 (1-ounce) squares semisweet
    chocolate, melted and cooled

⅓ cup whipping cream

2 cups frozen whipped topping,
    thawed

3 (1.55-ounce) milk chocolate
    with crisped rice bars, finely
    chopped

Garnishes: additional milk
    chocolate with crisped rice bars,
    chocolate shavings

Combine butter and 1 ounce chocolate in a medium saucepan. Cook over medium-low heat, stirring frequently, until melted. Remove from heat, and stir in crushed pretzels, pecans, and 3 tablespoons sugar. Press mixture firmly in bottom and 2 inches up sides of a 9-inch springform pan. Bake at 350° for 5 minutes. Let cool on a wire rack.

Beat cream cheese at medium speed of an electric mixer 2 minutes. Gradually add ⅔ cup sugar, beating well. Add eggs, one at a time, beating just until blended after each addition. Add melted chocolate and whipping cream; beat at low speed until blended. Pour batter into prepared crust. Bake at 375° for 35 minutes or until center is almost set. Let cool to room temperature on a wire rack. Cover and chill 8 hours.

Combine whipped topping and chopped candy bars, stirring gently. Spread over cheesecake. Cover and chill until ready to serve. Remove sides of pan. Garnish, if desired. Yield: one 9-inch cheesecake.

Easy Roasted Nut Clusters

3 cups hazelnuts

3 tablespoons butter or margarine

6 (2-ounce) squares vanilla-flavored
    candy coating

¼ cup semisweet chocolate
    morsels

Place hazelnuts in an ungreased jellyroll pan. Bake at 350° for 15 minutes. Rub hazelnuts briskly with a towel to remove skins; discard skins. Coarsely chop hazelnuts. Melt butter in a large skillet over medium heat. Add hazelnuts, and toss to coat. Remove from heat; set aside.

Place candy coating in top of a double boiler; bring water to a boil. Reduce heat to low; cook until coating melts. Remove from heat. Cool 2 minutes.

Add hazelnuts, and stir until coated. Gently stir in chocolate morsels, creating a marbled effect.

Drop mixture by heaping tablespoonfuls onto wax paper. Let cool completely. Yield: 3½ dozen.

Frosted Fruitcake Bars

¾ cup butter or margarine, softened
⅔ cup firmly packed brown sugar
⅓ cup molasses
3 large eggs
1½ cups all-purpose flour
½ pound candied pineapple, finely chopped (about 1¼ cups)
½ pound red and green candied cherries, finely chopped (about 1¼ cups)
1 cup coarsely chopped walnuts
¾ cup golden raisins
¼ cup all-purpose flour
1 teaspoon ground allspice
Caramel Frosting

Beat butter at medium speed of an electric mixer until creamy; gradually add sugar, beating well. Add molasses and eggs, beating well. Stir in 1½ cups flour.

Combine candied fruit, walnuts, raisins, ¼ cup flour, and allspice; toss well. Stir mixture into batter. (Batter will be thick.)

Grease and flour a 13- x 9- x 2-inch pan; line with wax paper, and grease paper. Spread batter in pan. Bake at 325° for 30 to 35 minutes. Let cool in pan on a wire rack. Spread warm Caramel Frosting over fruitcake. Let stand 30 minutes. Cut into bars. Yield: 2½ dozen.

Caramel Frosting

¼ cup plus 2 tablespoons butter or margarine
1½ cups firmly packed brown sugar
¼ cup dark corn syrup
½ cup whipping cream
2½ cups coarsely chopped walnuts

Combine butter, brown sugar, and corn syrup in a large saucepan. Bring to a boil over medium heat, stirring frequently, until sugar dissolves. Cook, without stirring, until mixture reaches hard ball stage (260°). Remove from heat.

Stir in whipping cream and walnuts. Return to heat, and cook just until mixture reaches soft ball stage (240°). Remove from heat, and let cool 1 minute. Yield: 3 cups.

Stained Glass Divinity

2½ cups sugar
½ cup light corn syrup
½ cup water
2 egg whites
1 teaspoon vanilla extract
½ cup toasted, chopped pecans
2 (.9-ounce) rolls multicolored hard candies, broken into pieces

Combine first 3 ingredients in a large saucepan or Dutch oven; cook over low heat, stirring constantly, until sugar dissolves. Cover and cook over medium heat minutes to wash down sugar crystals from sides of pan.

Uncover and cook over medium heat, without stirring, until mixture reaches hardball stage (260°).

Beat egg whites in a large bowl at high speed of a heavy-duty electric mixer until stiff peaks form.

Pour hot syrup mixture in a very thin stream over beaten egg whites, beating constantly at high speed. Add syrup more rapidly towards the end. Add vanilla, and continue beating until mixture loses i oss and holds its shape (about 5 minutes). uickly stir in pecans. Spread mixture into greased 8-inch square pan. Sprinkle mediately with crushed candy. Let stand room temperature until firm enough to t. Cut divinity into 1-inch squares. eld: 1¾ pounds.

Toasted Almond And Cranberry Cookies

½ cup butter or margarine, softened
½ cup shortening
1 cup firmly packed brown sugar
⅔ cup sugar
2 large eggs
2 cups all-purpose flour
1 teaspoon baking powder
½ teaspoon baking soda
⅛ teaspoon salt
8 ounces premium white chocolate, chopped
2 cups corn flakes cereal
1 cup sliced almonds, lightly toasted
2 (3-ounce) packages dried cranberries
¾ teaspoon almond extract

Beat butter and shortening at medium eed of an electric mixer until fluffy. radually add sugars, beating well. Add gs, mixing well. Add flour, baking powder, da, and salt. Stir in chocolate, cereal, monds, cranberries, and almond extract. Drop dough by tablespoonfuls 2 inches art onto ungreased cookie sheets. Bake at 0° for 10 minutes. Cool on wire racks. eld: 6 dozen.

Benne Seed Brittle

2 cups sugar
½ cup light corn syrup
½ cup boiling water
1¼ cups cashews, toasted and coarsely chopped
1 (2⅛-ounce) jar sesame seeds (about ½ cup), toasted
3 tablespoons butter or margarine
1 teaspoon baking soda
1 teaspoon vanilla extract

Combine first 3 ingredients in a heavy saucepan. Cook over medium heat, stirring constantly, until sugar dissolves. Cover and cook over medium heat 3 minutes to wash down sugar crystals from sides of pan. Uncover and cook, stirring occasionally, until mixture reaches hard crack stage (300°). Remove from heat, and stir in cashews and remaining ingredients.

Working rapidly, pour mixture onto a lightly buttered 15- x 10- x 1-inch jellyroll pan; spread in a thin layer. Let cool completely; break into large pieces. Store in airtight container. Yield: 1½ pounds.

Nutty Favors

✦ Send each guest home with small containers of mixed nuts.
✦ Share ideas for unique cookie packaging. (See page 137 for additional ideas.)

Winter Wonderland Sing-Along

Serves 12

Bacon and Cheese Roll-Ups

Broccoli Bites

Snowballs

Chocolate Mint Pillows

"Doe-a-Deer" Sugar Cookies

Rich Velvet Punch or
Cinnamon Cider

Hot Chocolate

Gather the neighbors together for an evening of singing around the piano or caroling out in the snow. Place a sled, plaid scarf, and other hints of the holiday season at your front door to set the mood. Plug in the tree lights, and serve these mouth-watering snacks and sweets as guests warm up in front of a roaring fire. The scent of Cinnamon Cider perking will fill your home with a heavenly aroma.

This assortment of holiday snacks, sweets, and warm beverages will delight guests of all ages.

Bacon and Cheese Roll-Ups

1 (8-ounce) package cream cheese
    with chives and onion
½ cup (2 ounces) finely shredded
    Cheddar cheese
¼ cup finely chopped natural
    almonds, toasted
3 tablespoons orange marmalade
24 slices bacon
48 rectangular-shaped buttery
    crackers

Combine first 4 ingredients in a small bowl; stir well. Cover and chill thoroughly.

Cook bacon in batches in a large skillet over medium heat 2 to 3 minutes on each side or until lightly browned; drain well on paper towels. Spread 1 level tablespoon cheese mixture on each of 24 crackers. Top each with another cracker. Wrap a slice bacon around each cracker stack, overlaping bacon ends on bottom. Place, sea side down, on ungreased baking shee Bake at 350° for 15 minutes or until bac is crisp. Serve immediately. Yield: 2 dozen

Snacks and Song

◆ *Pop these bacon-flavored snacks in the oven as guests arrive so they can enjoy a hot appetizer.*

◆ *Make copies of Christmas carols on heavy paper; place in a basket to distribute to guests for the sing-along.*

Broccoli Bites

1 small onion, chopped
1 clove garlic, minced
2 tablespoons vegetable oil
1 (10-ounce) package frozen
    chopped broccoli, thawed
6 large eggs, beaten
2½ cups (10 ounces) shredded
    Gouda cheese
⅓ cup Italian-seasoned breadcrum
1 (2-ounce) jar diced pimiento,
    drained
¾ teaspoon dried oregano
½ teaspoon pepper
¼ cup sesame seeds
⅓ cup grated Parmesan cheese

Cook onion and garlic in oil in a lar skillet over medium-high heat, stirring co stantly, until tender. Add broccoli, and co just until crisp-tender. Remove from heat.

Combine eggs and next 5 ingredients a large bowl, stirring well. Stir in broc mixture. Spoon mixture into a light greased 13- x 9- x 2-inch baking dish.

Toast sesame seeds in a small skillet ov high heat, stirring constantly, 2 minutes until golden. Sprinkle sesame seeds a Parmesan cheese over broccoli mixture.

Bake, uncovered, at 350° for 20 to 2 minutes or until browned. Let stand minutes. Cut into small squares, and ser warm. Yield: 3 dozen.

Snowballs

2¼ cups chocolate sandwich cookie crumbs
1 cup toasted, finely chopped pecans
1½ cups sifted powdered sugar, divided
⅓ cup flaked coconut
¼ cup light corn syrup
¼ cup strawberry preserves

Combine cookie crumbs, pecans, ¾ cup powdered sugar, and coconut in a bowl; stir well. Add corn syrup and preserves; stir well.

Shape mixture into balls, using 1 level tablespoon of mixture for each. Roll balls in remaining ¾ cup powdered sugar; roll again to coat well. Store in an airtight container up to 4 days. Yield: 28 cookies.

Chocolate Mint Pillows

1 (8-ounce) package cream cheese, softened
⅔ cup butter or margarine, softened
2½ cups all-purpose flour
½ cup sifted powdered sugar
2 (4.67-ounce) packages chocolate-covered mint wafer candies
1 tablespoon plus 1 teaspoon whipping cream

Beat cream cheese and butter at medium speed of an electric mixer until creamy. Gradually add flour and sugar, beating until blended. Divide dough in half; wrap in wax paper, and chill thoroughly.

Working with 1 portion of dough at a time, roll dough between 2 sheets of wax paper into an 18- x 8-inch rectangle. Remove top sheet of wax paper. Cut dough into 18 (4- x 2-inch) rectangles. Place a mint candy close to 1 end of each rectangle of dough. Fold dough over to enclose candy and form a small pillow.

Seal edges of dough securely with a fork. Repeat procedure with remaining half of dough. Place on ungreased cookie sheets. Bake at 375° for 12 to 14 minutes. Let cool on wire racks.

Combine remaining 20 mint wafer candies and whipping cream in top of a double boiler; bring water to a boil. Reduce heat to low; cook until candy melts and mixture is smooth, stirring frequently.

Spoon mint candy mixture into a zip-top plastic bag or a decorating bag fitted with a No. 2 round tip; seal bag, and if using a zip-top bag, snip a tiny hole in 1 corner, using scissors. Drizzle melted chocolate mixture over cookies. Yield: 3 dozen.

Edible and Ivory

◆ Snowballs and Chocolate Mint Pillows (above) offer a surprise filling that will delight the young-at-heart.

◆ Hire a pianist to "tickle the ivories" for your group.

"Doe-a-Deer" Sugar Cookies

1 cup butter, softened
1½ cups sugar
1 large egg
3⅓ cups all-purpose flour
½ teaspoon baking soda
½ teaspoon salt
1 teaspoon cream of tartar
2 teaspoons vanilla extract
Red sugar crystals
Red cinnamon candies

Beat butter at medium speed of an electric mixer 2 minutes or until soft and creamy. Gradually add sugar, beating well. Add egg, and beat well. Combine flou[r] soda, salt, and cream of tartar; add to bu[t]ter mixture, beating at low speed just unt[il] blended. Stir in vanilla. Shape dough into [a] ball. (Dough may be slightly crumbly.)

Roll dough to ¼-inch thickness on wa[x] paper. Cut with a 3½-inch reindeer-shape[d] cookie cutter, and place 2 inches apart o[n] ungreased cookie sheets. Sprinkle doug[h] with red sugar crystals. Place 1 cinnamo[n] candy on each reindeer for an eye.

Bake at 350° for 12 minutes or unt[il] edges of cookies are golden. Remove cook[ies] to wire racks to cool. Yield: 32 cookies.

Scents of the Season

✦ *Cinnamon Cider served in holiday mugs and "Doe-a-Deer" Sugar Cookies will fill tummies.*

✦ *Pass out mittens, scarves, and hats to the young ones in the crowd before caroling outdoors.*

Rich Velvet Punch

6 cups brewed coffee
3 cups half-and-half
1 cup Cookies 'n' Cream liqueur
¾ cup chocolate syrup
1 pint coffee ice cream

Combine first 4 ingredients in a larg[e] saucepan; stir well. Cook over medium he[at] until thoroughly heated. Add ice crean[m] stirring until ice cream melts. Serve warn[m] Yield: 3 quarts.

Cinnamon Cider

1½ quarts apple cider
1 quart cranberry-apple drink
2 cups pineapple juice
¾ cup red cinnamon candies
2 teaspoons whole cloves
Cinnamon sticks (optional)

Pour first 3 ingredients into an electr[ic] percolator. Place cinnamon candies an[d] cloves in percolator basket. Perk throug[h] complete cycle of percolator. Serve hot wit[h] cinnamon stick stirrers, if desired. Yiel[d] 3 quarts.

Creative Cookie Packaging

Try these innovative yet easy ways to dress up cookies and candies for holiday gift giving.

Line a gift bag with colored tissue paper; fill with cookies. Using fabric paint, stamp a child's handprint onto a pot holder. Attach ribbon and a gift tag.

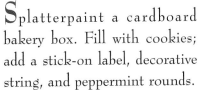

Splatterpaint a cardboard bakery box. Fill with cookies; add a stick-on label, decorative string, and peppermint rounds.

Glue wrapping paper or contact paper around an empty potato chip can. Fill with cookies, and add candy canes, a bow, and a gift tag.

Purchase an antique teacup at a tag sale. Tie goodies in plastic wrap with ribbon. Add a sprig of greenery and a gift tag.

Place a bag of cookies in an inexpensive wicker birdcage. Thread ribbon around cage. Add a sprig of greenery and a handmade bird-shaped tag.

Glue wide ribbon onto small empty coffee tins. Add cookies. Stack tins, and tie them together with ribbon. Add greenery and gift tags.

Christmas Day Brunch

Serves 4

Eggnog French Toast Sticks

Sausage or Bacon

Favorite Ambrosia

White Christmas Tree

Fruit Juice   Coffee

Awaken on this magical day
to a midmorning treat.
Hang a stocking full of goodies on the back of
each family member's chair. Place an edible
Christmas tree in the center of your
breakfast table, and enjoy a cup of coffee while
the kids eat the bite-size doughnuts from
the tree. Invite your neighbors over for
doughnuts, or triple the menu if serving a
larger crowd. Spoon up bowls of ambrosia, and
serve it with this quick French toast.

Eggnog French Toast Sticks, sausage, Favorite Ambrosia,
White Christmas Tree (recipes on following pages)

Eggnog French Toast Sticks

8 (1-inch-thick) slices French bread
  or sourdough bread
1 cup commercial or homemade
  eggnog
½ teaspoon ground nutmeg
¼ cup butter or margarine,
  divided
  Sifted powdered sugar

**Midmorning
Magic**

◆ For an eye-
opener, start the
day with Eggnog
French Toast
Sticks, sausage,
and Favorite
Ambrosia (right).
◆ An edible
doughnut tree
(far right) makes
a whimsical
centerpiece.

Cut French bread slices into 1-inch-wide strips. Set bread aside. Combine eggnog and nutmeg in a shallow bowl. Preheat griddle to 350°; melt 2 tablespoons butter on griddle.

Dip bread strips in eggnog mixture, one at a time. Cook, a few at a time, 2 to 4 minutes on each side or until golden, adding additional 2 tablespoons butter to griddle as needed.

Sprinkle French toast lightly with powdered sugar. Serve French toast immediately with syrup. Yield: 4 servings.

Favorite Ambrosia

3 oranges
2 grapefruit
1 large banana, sliced
½ cup coarsely chopped maraschino
  cherries
2 tablespoons salad dressing or
  mayonnaise
1 tablespoon powdered sugar
¼ teaspoon grated orange rind
¾ cup frozen whipped topping,
  thawed
¼ cup flaked coconut, toasted
  Garnish: maraschino cherries
  with stems

Peel and section oranges and grapefruit, catching juice in a bowl. Toss banana slices in fruit juice, and remove with a slotted spoon. Place grapefruit sections in a small glass bowl. Layer orange sections, chopped cherries, and banana slices over grapefruit. Pour juice over layered fruit.

Combine salad dressing, sugar, and orange rind; fold in whipped topping. Spoon over fruit; sprinkle with coconut. Garnish, if desired. Yield: 4 servings.

White Christmas Tree

White Christmas Tree

1 (10-inch) plastic foam cone
3 dozen powdered sugar-coated
  small doughnuts
  Fresh cranberries
  Fresh mint sprigs (optional)

Position foam cone on a pedestal or serving plate covered with a white doily. Insert wooden picks into cone about 1 inch apart. Place a doughnut on each wooden pick, covering entire cone.

Place cranberries on additional wooden picks, and insert into cone between doughnuts. Decorate tree with fresh mint sprigs, if desired. Display cone as an edible centerpiece. Yield: 1 doughnut tree.

New Year's Eve Resolutions Party

Serves 16

Cheese Terrine

Black-Eyed Caviar

Mushroom-Port Phyllo Purses

Tortellini Toss

Kahlúa Truffle Sticks

Champagne   Wine   Coffee

Ring in the new year with the ones you love, accompanied by a fabulous display of food and fun. Fill your home with a lively group of friends and a vibrant table decorated with clocks and bells. You won't be at a loss for games at this party— toss New Year's resolutions and predictions into a decorative basket; then draw at random, and guess who said what.

From left: Mushroom-Port Phyllo Purses (page 145), Black-Eyed Caviar (page 145), Tortellini Toss (page 146)

Cheese Terrine

¼ cup Chablis or other dry
   white wine
1 pound provolone cheese, cut into
   ¹⁄₁₆-inch-thick slices
   Pesto Filling
   Walnut-Goat Cheese Filling
   Sun-Dried Tomato Filling
1 (15-ounce) jar marinara sauce
   Italian bread
   Garnishes: fresh basil leaves,
   walnut halves

Cut a single piece of cheesecloth to fit into a 4-cup ring mold; dampen with wine, gently squeezing out excess moisture. Line mold with cheesecloth, allowing excess to extend over rim.

Cut provolone cheese slices in half. Line bottom and sides of mold with half of cheese slices. Divide remaining cheese into 3 equal portions; set aside.

Spoon Pesto Filling over cheese in ring mold. Top with one-third of remaining cheese slices. Spoon Walnut-Goat Cheese Filling over cheese; layer another one-third cheese slices on top. Spoon Sun-Dried Tomato Filling over cheese, spreading gently to edges; top with remaining cheese slices. Fold cheesecloth over top, and press lightly. Cover and chill 8 hours.

Unfold cheesecloth, and invert terri[ne] onto a serving platter. Discard cheesecloth

To serve, cut terrine into 1-inch slice[s]. Serve with marinara sauce on Italian brea[d] slices. Garnish, if desired. Yield: 16 app[e]tizer servings.

Pesto Filling

1 cup firmly packed fresh basil
   leaves
1 cup freshly grated Parmesan
   cheese
½ cup olive oil
2 cloves garlic, sliced

Combine all ingredients in container [of] an electric blender. Cover and process un[til] almost smooth, scraping down sides of co[n]tainer occasionally. Yield: 1 cup.

Walnut-Goat Cheese Filling

1 cup crumbled goat cheese
⅔ cup toasted, chopped
   walnuts
¼ cup sour cream
1 clove garlic, sliced

Combine all ingredients in container [of] an electric blender. Cover and process un[til] almost smooth, scraping down sides of co[n]tainer occasionally. Yield: 1¼ cups.

Sun-Dried Tomato Filling

1 (7-ounce) jar oil-packed
   sun-dried tomatoes, undrained
1 cup freshly grated Parmesan
   cheese
2 teaspoons lemon juice

Combine all ingredients in container [of] an electric blender. Cover and process un[til] almost smooth, scraping sides of contain[er] occasionally. Yield: 1¼ cups.

Black-Eyed Caviar

2 (15-ounce) cans black-eyed peas, drained
1 yellow or green pepper, finely chopped
½ cup roasted red pepper packed in oil, drained and finely chopped
½ cup minced purple onion
½ cup minced fresh cilantro or parsley
¼ cup olive oil
2 cloves garlic, minced
2 tablespoons white wine vinegar
1 teaspoon ground cumin
2 teaspoons coarse-grained mustard
¼ teaspoon salt

Combine all ingredients in a medium-ize bowl; stir well. Cover and chill several ours. Serve at room temperature with pita hips. Yield: 4½ cups.

Mushroom-Port Phyllo Purses

1 (⅞-ounce) package dried shiitake mushrooms (¾ cup)
1 cup port wine
½ pound fresh mushrooms, chopped
¼ cup butter or margarine, melted
½ teaspoon dried thyme
½ cup soft cream cheese
¼ cup minced fresh chives
12 sheets frozen phyllo pastry, thawed
⅓ cup butter or margarine, melted
   Freshly ground pepper
   Vegetable cooking spray
   Blanched whole chives (optional)

Combine dried mushrooms and wine in a small saucepan; bring to a boil. Cover, remove from heat, and let mushroom mixture stand 30 minutes.

Drain mushrooms, reserving wine; finely chop mushrooms. Strain wine through a coffee filter into a small bowl; reserve strained liquid and mushrooms.

Combine fresh mushrooms, ¼ cup butter, and thyme in a large skillet. Cook over medium-high heat 15 to 20 minutes or until liquid is absorbed, stirring frequently. Add reserved liquid and dried mushrooms; simmer, uncovered, for 10 minutes, or until liquid is absorbed. Remove from heat; let cool, and stir in cream cheese and chives.

Place 1 sheet of phyllo on wax paper. Brush lightly with melted butter. Layer 2 more sheets of phyllo on top, brushing each lightly with melted butter. Using kitchen scissors, cut layers into 9 rectangles. Place 1 level tablespoon of mushroom mixture in center of each phyllo rectangle. Sprinkle lightly with pepper.

Gather corners of phyllo over the filling, and gently twist to close pastry. Lightly spray outside with cooking spray. Place on an ungreased baking sheet. Repeat procedure with remaining phyllo sheets and mushroom mixture.

Bake at 350° for 12 to 15 minutes or until golden. Tie a blanched chive around top of each purse, if desired. Serve hot or at room temperature. Yield: 3 dozen.

Champagne and Caviar

✦ *Black-Eyed Caviar (left) provides a rainbow of color, and, of course, that traditional dose of good luck.*

✦ *Painted plastic champagne flutes make memorable party favors—fill with bubbly for a midnight toast to the New Year.*

Tortellini Toss

2 teaspoons cumin seeds
1 tablespoon fennel seeds
½ pound unsliced pepperoni, cut into ¾-inch cubes
1 (7-ounce) jar oil-packed sun-dried tomatoes
3 tablespoons Dijon mustard
3 large cloves garlic, sliced
½ cup olive oil
½ cup slivered almonds, toasted
1½ tablespoons lemon juice
2 pounds fresh cheese-filled spinach tortellini
1 large sweet yellow or sweet red pepper, cut into 1-inch pieces
1 (6-ounce) can whole pitted ripe olives, drained
1 pint cherry tomatoes, halved

Place cumin and fennel seeds in a skillet; place over medium heat, shaking skillet often, until seeds are lightly browned and fragrant. Remove from heat, and let cool.

Position knife blade in food processor bowl; add seeds, half of pepperoni, and next 3 ingredients. Cover and process until smooth. With processor running, pour olive oil through food chute in a slow, steady stream. Add almonds and lemon juice; process until almonds are finely chopped and mixture is blended.

Cook tortellini according to package directions; drain. Combine tortellini, remaining pepperoni, pepper, and olives in a large serving bowl. Add pepperoni sauce, and toss well. Gently stir in halved tomatoes. To serve, provide long wooden skewers for spearing. Yield: 16 appetizer servings.

Kahlúa Truffle Sticks

2 tablespoons sugar
1 (4-ounce) bar Swiss dark chocolate, chopped
3 (1-ounce) squares unsweetened chocolate, chopped
¼ cup plus 2 tablespoons butter or margarine, softened and divided
¾ cup sugar
2 large eggs
⅔ cup all-purpose flour
¼ teaspoon salt
⅓ cup Kahlúa
½ cup semisweet chocolate mini-morsels

Line a greased 8-inch square pan with foil, allowing foil to extend over edges. Butter foil; sprinkle 2 tablespoons sugar onto foil.

Combine chopped chocolate and 2 tablespoons butter in top of a double boiler; bring water to a boil. Reduce heat to low; cook until chocolate and butter melt. Remove from heat, and let cool.

Beat remaining ¼ cup butter at medium speed of an electric mixer 2 minutes. Gradually add ¾ cup sugar, beating at medium speed 5 minutes. Add eggs, one at a time, beating until blended.

Combine flour and salt; add to butter mixture alternately with melted chocolate mixture and Kahlúa, beginning and ending with flour mixture. Mix at low speed just until blended. Stir in mini-morsels.

Spoon batter into prepared pan. Bake at 350° for 18 minutes (do not overbake). Cool completely. Cover and chill at least 2 hours. To serve, lift foil out of pan, and cut into 2- x 1-inch sticks. Yield: 32 brownies.

Famous Last Words

Relish these words of wisdom
from years past as you plan your own toast to the New Year.

Now the New Year comes and the
Old takes flight;
Dear God of our years, be close
tonight!
—*Mary Baldwin*

Beautiful is the year in its
coming and in its going.
—*Lucy Larcom*

The Old Year's heart its hopes laid
down,
As in a grave; but, trusting, said:
"The flowers of the New Year's
crown
Bloom from the ashes of the dead."
—*Helen Hunt Jackson*

Even while we sing, he smiles
his last,
And leaves our sphere behind.
The good Old Year is with the past,
O be the New as kind!
—*William Cullen Bryant*

Another year, with tears and joys,
To form the arch of love;
Another year to toil with hope,
And seek for rest above.
—*Thomas O'Hagan*

Ring out the old, ring in the new,
Ring, happy bells, across the snow:
The year is going, let him go;
Ring out the false, ring in the true.
—*Alfred Tennyson*

I see not a step before me as I tread
on another year;
But I've left the Past in God's
keeping—the Future His mercy
shall clear;
And what looks dark in the
distance, may brighten as I
draw near.
—*Mary Gardiner Brainard*

A casket with its gifts concealed—
This is the Year that for you waits
Beyond tomorrow's mystic gates.
—*Horatio Nelson Powers*

Let the ills we met,
And the sad regret,
With the Old be buried deep;
For what joy untold
Doth the New Year hold,
And what hopes within it sleep!
—*George Cooper*

Who comes dancing over the snow,
His soft little feet all bare and
rosy?
Open the door, though the wild
winds blow,
Take the child in and make him
cozy.
Take him in and hold him dear,
He is the wonderful glad New
Year.
—*Dinah Maria Mulock Craik*

The merry year is born
Like the bright berry from the
naked thorn.
—*Hartley Coleridge*

The New Year enters in: a happy
child,
Who looks for flowers to fill
her outstretched hand,
And knows not fear although the
winds be wild.
—*Mary Gorges*

I asked the New Year, "What am I
to do
The whole year through?"
The answer came,
"Be true."
—*Grace Noll Crowell*

Time is like a fashionable host,
That slightly shakes his parting
guest by th' hand,
But with his arms outstretch'd,
as he would fly,
Grasps in the comer: Welcome
ever smiles,
And Farewell goes out sighing.
—*Shakespeare*

Good-bye, Old Year! Tried, trusty
friend,
thy tale at last is told;
O New Year! write thou thine
for us in lines of brightest gold.
—*Unknown*

Dost thou love life? Then waste
not time,
for time is the stuff that life is
made of.
—*Benjamin Franklin*

Valentine's Sweetheart Surprises

German Chocolate Fudge Hearts

Cupid's White Chocolate Brownie

Cornucopia Filled with Hugs® and Kisses™

Present your sweetheart with one of these enticing gifts of food. They're all easily prepared, and the unique packaging ideas and presentations make them memorable. Tie a ribbon around the chocolate-coated cornucopia full of candy, or present Cupid's White Chocolate Brownie heart in a pizza box spray-painted white and smothered in kisses. You'll never again have to worry whether you've captured your valentine's heart.

German Chocolate Fudge Hearts

¼ cup plus 2 tablespoons butter or
  margarine
1 (4-ounce) bar sweet baking
  chocolate
⅔ cup sugar
1 large egg
1 tablespoon vanilla extract
1 cup all-purpose flour
¼ teaspoon salt
¾ cup flaked coconut

Melt butter and chocolate in a heavy saucepan over low heat, stirring frequently. Remove from heat; stir in sugar. Add egg, stirring just until blended. Stir in vanilla.

Combine flour and salt. Add flour mixture to chocolate mixture; stir well. Stir in coconut. Spoon batter into 10 greased and floured 3-inch heart-shaped ovenproof molds, filling three-fourths full.

Bake at 375° for 12 to 14 minutes. Let cool 10 minutes in molds. Remove from molds, and let cool on a wire rack.

Wrap fudge hearts in a decorative airtight container, and tie with ribbon. Yield: 1 (3-inch) hearts.

Variation: To make 1 (8-inch) German Chocolate Fudge Heart, spoon batter into greased and floured 8-inch heart-shaped cakepan. Bake at 375° for 20 minutes or until a wooden pick inserted in center comes out clean. Let cool 10 minutes; remove from pan. Cool on a wire rack.

Heartfelt Fudge

◆ *Sliced almonds outline Cupid's White Chocolate Brownie (at right in box). Line the gift box with colored tissue paper.*
◆ *Stack these decadent fudgy hearts (right) in an acrylic canister. Glue assorted valentine candies on the outside for decoration.*

Cupid's White Chocolate Brownie

⅓ cup butter or margarine
8 ounces white chocolate, chopped and divided
2 large eggs
⅔ cup sugar
1 cup all-purpose flour
½ teaspoon baking powder
¼ teaspoon salt
1 tablespoon vanilla extract
¼ cup sliced almonds

Grease bottom and sides of an 8-inch heart-shaped cakepan; line bottom with parchment paper. Grease parchment paper. Set aside.

Melt butter in a small saucepan over low heat. Add half of white chocolate, and remove from heat. (Do not stir.)

Beat eggs at medium speed of an electric mixer until thick and pale; gradually add sugar, beating well. Combine flour, baking powder, and salt; add to egg mixture, mixing just until blended. Stir in melted butter mixture and vanilla. Fold in remaining chopped white chocolate.

Spoon mixture into prepared pan. Place almonds around edge of pan, overlapping to form a border. Bake at 350° for 30 to 35 minutes. Let cool in pan 10 minutes. Remove from pan, and let cool completely on a wire rack. Yield: one 8-inch heart-shaped brownie.

Cornucopia Filled With Hugs® and Kisses™

1 large waffle cone (about 7 inches long)
2 (2-ounce) squares chocolate-flavored candy coating
2 teaspoons shortening
12 milk chocolate pieces with almonds
12 solid white chocolate and milk chocolate pieces

Place waffle cone, pointed end up, on a small wire rack over wax paper. (If waffle cone opening is uneven, place a small measuring cup under cone to balance it.)

Combine candy coating and shortening in top of a double boiler; bring water to a boil. Reduce heat to low; cook until candy coating melts, stirring frequently. Remove from heat, leaving coating over hot water.

Slowly spoon candy coating over waffle cone on rack, coating evenly. Let stand 15 to 20 minutes or until chocolate is set. Repeat coating procedure, if desired.

To serve, fill chocolate cornucopia with milk chocolate and white chocolate pieces. Yield: 1 serving.

Note: Cornucopia may be coated ahead and stored in an airtight container up to 5 days. Cornucopia may also be filled with a scoop of your favorite ice cream or other types of valentine candy.

Acknowledgments

Oxmoor House wishes to thank the following individuals and merchants:

Archipelago, New York, NY
Attic Antiques, Birmingham, AL
Mrs. Alison Turner Bachofer
Birmingham Antique Mall, Inc., Birmingham, AL
Bridges Antiques, Birmingham, AL
Bromberg and Company, Inc., Birmingham, AL
Cassis and Company, New York, NY
The Chinaberry, Birmingham, AL
Christine's, Birmingham, AL
Custom Sign Express, Birmingham, AL
Don Drennen Buick Jeep Eagle, Birmingham, AL
Mr. and Mrs. James Edwards
Frankie Engel Antiques, Birmingham, AL
Fitz and Floyd, Dallas, TX
Mrs. Katherine Hamilton
The Holly Tree, Inc., Birmingham, AL
Ms. Ashley Johnson
Mrs. Judy Leesburg
Michelle's, Birmingham, AL
Old World Pewter, Mount Pleasant, SC
Reed and Barton, Taunton, MA
Stonefish Pottery, Providence, RI
Mr. Corey Troiano
Union Street Glass, Oakland, CA
Vietri, Hillsborough, NC
Villeroy & Boch, Arlington, VA
Maralyn Wilson Gallery, Birmingham, AL

Locations

Mr. and Mrs. Richard M. Baker
Bridges Antiques, Birmingham, AL
Dr. and Mrs. Mark Clark
Mr. and Mrs. Peter J. Clemens, III
Mr. and Mrs. Gordon W. Miller
Mr. and Mrs. William O. Mooney, Jr.
Perdido Beach Resort, Orange Beach, AL
Mr. Tom Rasinen
Mr. Michael Stephens and the Resting S Ranch
Mr. Steve Watkins
Dr. and Mrs. Ernest C. Wood
Dr. and Mrs. H. Evan Zeiger, Jr.

Contributing Recipe Developer

Debby Maugans, pages 27, 30-31, 52-53, 112-115, 144-146

HUGS and KISSES are trademarks and used with permission of Hershey Foods Corporation.

Recipe Index

page 21

page 65

page 12

$\mathcal{S}$ubject Index

page 106

page 80

page 117